Positive Training for Show Dogs
Building a Relationship for Success

Vicki Ronchette

Publishing

Wenatchee, Washington U.S.A.

Positive Training for Show Dogs
Building a Relationship for Success
Vicki Ronchette

Dogwise Publishing
A Division of Direct Book Service, Inc.
701B Poplar Wenatchee, Washington 98807
1-509-663-9115, 1-800-776-2665
www.dogwisepublishing.com / info@dogwisepublishing.com

© 2008 Victoria Ronchette

Graphic Design: Nathan Woodward
Indexing: Cheryl Smith
Photographs: Vicki Ronchette, Rick Ronchette, Georgie Hesse, Alan and Melissa Reyes, Karen Fink, Jennifer Anderson, Lisa Clifton-Bumpass and Warren Cook of Fox and Cook Photography.

Cataloging-in-Publication Data is available upon request from the Library of Congress
ISBN: 1-929242-46-8 3770 2171   7/08
Printed in the U.S.A.

TABLE OF CONTENTS

For Donna and Boris

Introduction

Dog training is continuously changing and evolving all the time. When I started showing dogs more than a decade ago, very few people, myself included, had heard of "positive reinforcement" or "clicker training." Sure, we used treats some of the time, but we also depended on leash pops, corrections, and other methods that are now considered too harsh. Those were the methods I was taught, and I am sure it is the same for many dog-show people. While I managed to finish championships and earn obedience titles on dogs using these methods, I have since found a better way to train.

Over the years, as I began to read books and attend seminars and workshops that promoted positive training methods, I came to have a clearer understanding of learning theory and why training using positive techniques is beneficial to show dogs. I learned to use that knowledge to train dogs to be more reliable and—in the end—bring greater success in the ring. The results include happier dogs, happier handlers, and healthier canine/human relationships.

Since I implemented positive training methods, I have had increased success with my dogs. I communicate better with them and they give me more in and out of the ring. My dogs no longer seem confused, bored or difficult to handle. Show dogs must enjoy showing to be successful. That's why we teach them—not force them—to enjoy what we want them to do.

Enjoyment is too often missing at dog shows—for dogs and their handlers. I see people jerk, pull, push and force dogs to show for them. I see stressed dogs outside the ring with handlers who seem unaware or unconcerned about their emotional state. I see frightened and shy dogs forced to "deal with it." I see dogs whose handlers think they "shouldn't get away with it." I wonder what it is that they think a terrified dog is "getting away with?" A frightened dog isn't getting away with anything. The showing experience isn't fun for those dogs and, dogs that aren't having fun, don't win. Showing dogs should be about the dogs first and the wins second. Anyone who values the ribbons and trophies more than the dog should find another hobby that doesn't involve a living animal.

I also see people at dog shows who are nervous, frustrated and angry, especially if they aren't getting results. They try to be gentle and kind, but when that doesn't work the tension can be overwhelming. This in turn makes the dog frightened or afraid when it should be receiving guidance and help. Too many handlers plod along showing dogs who don't enjoy it. They need help, but do not know where to find it.

When I decided to use a clicker to train my show dogs, there was no information available. Books on clicker training or e-mail lists on the subject did not exist, and even today the information is sketchy for people who wish to use positive methods to train their show dogs.

That is why I decided to write this book.

I will teach you, step by step, how to prepare your dog for the show ring using a clicker and other positive methods. You will learn how to put these behaviors on command so that you don't need the clicker or food in the ring. I will show you how to solve problems that your dog may have in the show ring. And, I am going to share with you how I helped my own dogs, and my clients' dogs, solve show ring problems such as helping frightened or shy dogs overcome fears and anxieties.

Throughout this book, I will encourage you to try new training methods. Perhaps you are curious about clicker training a show dog, but don't know how to get started. You will find positive methods particularly helpful if you have a dog who is considered "soft," has reacted poorly to corrections, is easily frightened, or is insecure. At times, I will challenge you to reconsider what you think is the "norm."

I assume that the reader of this book knows dog show basics: terminology, how to enter shows, and dog show etiquette. This is fundamentally a dog training book, but I have included a Resource section with a selection of good books to read on shows if you are a novice.

I believe that showing can be more enjoyable for dogs and their owners. I aim to help you find positive solutions to problems and I will help you become more creative and thoughtful in your training. Give it a shot and have fun with it. What have you got to lose?

Ribbon enjoying her first dog show

Chapter 1
DOG SHOWS AND SHOW DOGS

A dog show involves showing dogs to experienced judges who determine if a particular dog is worthy of a win. Dogs are judged on how well they conform to their official breed standards. Ultimately, several wins earn the dog a championship title, which is the goal of most people who show dogs. Often, fanciers will not breed their show dogs unless, or until, they earn a championship. Most show fanciers are interested in improving breeding stock, the end result being dogs who are bred to improve and preserve the integrity of a particular breed.

All breeds have a written standard that details their desired characteristics. This standard is the blueprint for what that breed should look like, as well as desired temperament or abilities of the breed. For example, a breed standard outlines how the tail and ears should be set, how tall the dog should be and how much it should weigh. It may even specify how many teeth the dog should have. These individual attributes of a dog come together to make a holistic, correct, picture of a particular breed.

More Than A Written Standard
A breed standard is what the dogs are supposed to be judged against. But breed standards are written words open to interpretation by judges. One particular standard states that the breed should be "low." That's it, just low. It doesn't give a specific number of inches for height. It is open to interpretation by the judge. Low can be interpreted different ways, by

different people. How low is low? Is low the same to you as it is to me? Although judges try to be objective, subjectivity is at work here.

And, consider this. Have you ever heard a judge or handler say, "This dog really showed well today?" How do you determine "showing well" since it is obviously subjective? Does the dog walk into the ring and demand that all eyes are focused on him? Does a bitch move as if to say, "Here I am, don't I look fabulous?" Like it or not, such factors do play a role in which dog wins on a particular day. Even if a dog is structurally sound and exceptional in quality for his breed, when he slumps around the ring with his head down as if to say, "I hate this," he is unlikely to be a top contender. I have seen fantastic dogs overlooked for this reason. I have known owners who decided to stop showing because the dog hated it so much. Showmanship for show dogs is important even though it is beyond the scope of a written standard.

Have you ever talked to someone after watching the Westminster dog show on television? Have you ever listened to non-dog people talk about it? If it was a particularly striking dog, a dog who demanded the win, covered ground confidently and then threw himself into a perfect free stack, even novices will say, "That dog really wanted to win." People who have never been to a dog show can see showmanship. It cannot be denied.

You Can Train Your Dog to Love Showing
Some dogs naturally love showing. They move with confidence and seem to enjoy being watched. For others, exhibiting doesn't come so easily. There are many fine dogs who have not finished a championship due to "lack of ring presence." In other words, they are sound, deserving and correct dogs, but they don't show well. It is as if they want to be invisible. It's a shame, but it is a reality of the show world.

A lack of ring presence is also true with performance dogs. Many great dogs never make it as top-level agility or obedience competitors because they do not enjoy the events at a trial. They slink around, apparently trying not to be seen. It always amazes me when owners are surprised that their agility dogs have a difficult time at trials. It's not that the dog won't perform, it's that he can't perform. The dog is not comfortable in a competitive environment.

Successful show dogs enjoy showing. If they aren't born loving it, they must be taught to love it. You can't teach dogs to love an activity by forcing or scaring them. You have to teach them by making it rewarding. Dogs don't care about championship titles or blue ribbons—those rewards are for the handler. Dogs need to be rewarded in ways that mean something to them. Your job is to learn how to make it rewarding for the dog.

My job is to help you learn to train your show dog in such a way that he will enjoy both the training process and—amazingly—participating in dog shows. The following positive techniques will help make show-ring training and showing a fun, rewarding game to the dog and more enjoyable for you.

Chapter 2
GOING POSITIVE

Most serious dog fanciers are aware that so-called "positive" dog training methods are popular. However, there are a lot of misconceptions about what "positive" means. Positive dog training focuses on using rewards to get desired behaviors rather than correcting undesirable behaviors. This sounds simple, but using positive training methods is actually the opposite of what many owners do with their dogs—and their spouses and children. It seems natural to correct a dog (or child) after he has done something wrong rather than waiting for an opportunity to reward him for doing something right. Going "positive" is not always an easy process, especially if you have found that corrections work. Let me share how I came to know that using positive training methods is better.

The Crossover Trainer
I am a "crossover trainer." This means that I started out training with force and corrections. When faced with a problem behavior, I would sometimes use punishment to correct it. I now focus on using positive reinforcement to encourage the behavior I want from a dog. Simply put, I used to train with corrections, now I do not. This doesn't mean that I don't take training seriously, or that I don't have high standards for my dogs or my clients' dogs. It means that I have learned what so many other trainers have learned over the last several years: there is a better way. There is a way to train dogs that makes it fun and challenging to the dog; a way that allows the dog to join in the learning process and offer behaviors in

exchange for rewards; a way for the dog to receive what he perceives as valuable while he learns behaviors you want him to learn; a way to teach the dog to enjoy showing. This process is fabulous to witness and, once most dog fanciers see it for themselves, they are thoroughly impressed with what dogs can do. Positive training brings out the best in my dogs, allowing them to shine in and out of the show ring.

Positive Reinforcement vs. Corrections

How is positive training different from training based on corrections? Positive training methods focus on providing positive reinforcement (or rewards) to the dog so a desired behavior will occur again. You give the dog something he finds rewarding when he does something you want him to do. If administered properly, the dog will perform a desired behavior for you more often. You focus on what you want the dog to do and reward and reinforce those behaviors instead of focusing on what he does "wrong." In a nutshell, that is positive training philosophy.

When corrections are used, the training is considered aversive. Aversive training means something that is unpleasant to the dog will occur if the dog does something the trainer does not want him to do. The level of aversion can be as minimal as a spray bottle full of water to deter dogs from barking or chewing the furniture. Using a water bottle to correct a dog is a technique that many owners feel comfortable with since it does not cause pain to the animal. Another mild form of aversive training is to use a commercial spray (such as Bitter Apple™ or Fooey™) to stop the dog from chewing on its bed, the couch or kitchen cabinets. Aversive methods that are considered harsh are shock collars or jerking the dog's neck with a choke chain.

Some trainers believe that aversive techniques (especially mild corrections such as the water bottle and taste deterrents) are effective and should be included in a training program. Other trainers think that any type of aversive is unkind, unfair, and ineffective. The truth is, no one is going to agree on this. I have talked to trainers all over the country and there continues to be controversy. There is no consensus on the best or most effective dog-training techniques. However, it is my opinion that the results you can achieve with positive techniques are much better and more reliable than what can be achieved with corrections.

My best advice is if it doesn't seem right, don't do it. If you are uncomfortable with it, don't do it. If it frightens or hurts your dog, I say find a better way. If it isn't working, then stop. I have no problem with an owner spraying Bitter Apple on her couch to discourage the dog from chewing. Verbal reprimands administered gently are acceptable once you have mastered positive techniques, though they are rarely needed. However, I would not work with an owner who wants to train with a shock or electronic collar because I am personally not comfortable with it (and it is most often not an effective long-term solution). Owners must decide individually what they believe is acceptable and what isn't.

A Personal Journey

The first dog who I ever set out to train seriously was Boris. Boris was a Rottweiler I acquired as an intact, unruly adolescent who had been abandoned. I had wanted a Rottweiler for a long time even though many are temperamentally unsound because they are not properly trained. Boris had been abandoned when his family moved away. His owners usually left him on a very tight choke chain and prong collar tied to an old porcelain sink or a tree in the backyard.

It took me thirty seconds to realize that this dog really needed training. Since there was a local dog-training club in the next town, I signed up for classes. After the first night of class, my hands were raw from Boris pulling on the lead while I struggled to hold onto to him with it. On the way home I cried and thought, "I can't do this. This is too hard." I felt better the next day and went to class again. Although I was uncomfortable with the recommendation to use a prong collar on Boris, I did. I was assured it would help, and indeed it did. It made all the difference in the world: power steering. We were taught to pop the leash when the dog was out of position and give praise and hot dog pieces when he did something correctly. Boris and I were on our way. Boris graduated second place in his class. I was very proud of him.

I continued to work with Boris and our relationship developed. He earned his CD (Companion Dog) title and a CGC (Canine Good Citizen) award. Boris was taught with a combination of corrections and praise. I know now that had he been trained with strictly positive methods he would have been a much more reliable dog, and he would have enjoyed the training a lot more. I continued to train him toward his CDX (Companion Dog Excellent) title. I became a regular at the dog-training club and even became an assistant trainer. I spent several years at the club at least two nights a week working the desk, assisting the trainer and training my dogs.

Though I did begin training Boris with corrections, I was fortunate to have been taught to use food as a reward. It really wasn't until I started working with other dogs that I discovered not all dogs are as resilient as Boris. Not many can shake off a correction like Boris could. Some dogs are more sensitive, and feel hurt or insecure with corrections. I also learned that certain dogs will shut down and stop wanting to work at all. I began to wonder if using corrections were the best way to train all dogs.

As I continued to wonder about this, I found a book by Karen Pryor on clicker training (*Getting Started with Clicker Training*) and decided to buy

Boris Badenov, CD, CGC.

it. I obtained an Australian Cattle Dog puppy with the specific purpose of training him using the clicker training methods I learned about in Pryor's book: no corrections, only a clicker. I chose a Cattle Dog for a number of reasons. First, I love the look and intelligence of the breed, and I wanted a breed that has been labeled "hard-headed" and that is traditionally trained fairly harshly so that I would really know if clicker-training was effective. I thought that if clicker training worked, I could use the Cattle Dog as a demo dog and owners could see if I could train my Cattle Dog with positive techniques, they could train their dogs, as well.

I began training Billy the Kid when he was six weeks old. I used only positive training techniques. Today, that Cattle Dog is the demo dog for all my classes. It is exciting and fun to watch, and hear owners "ooh" and "aahh" over how good he is. But, more importantly, watching Billy inspires owners to train their own dogs.

Billy at two years of age.

I am now training all my dogs using positive methods. My students are taught to train using positive reinforcement and the clicker. I train my dogs with their regular collars and encourage my students to do the same. It's a liberating feeling to have found a new way to train. I want to help and encourage owners who show dogs to step outside the box and try positive methods.

Even though I started out using aversive methods, I will never be ashamed of how I started or how I learned. I am very grateful to my early trainers who taught me so much about dogs and helped me to achieve the goals I set for myself. I am proud to have searched longer and harder to find techniques with which I am more comfortable. I try not to be judgmental of traditional trainers, and hope that one day they might be ready to challenge themselves to train differently.

I only wish Boris was still here to share this with me. I wish that I could have learned to train this way earlier so that we could have enjoyed each other even more.

So, I encourage you to give positive reinforcement training a shot. I cannot tell you how many students (including skilled, traditional trainers who are very skeptical about clicker training) are delighted and amazed with the results. Whether you want to train your new show prospect or work out a specific issue that has you stumped, this is the method for you. This method really is for everyone and every dog. Let's get started. You're going to love it!

Chapter 3

THE FOUNDATION IS
THE RELATIONSHIP

One of the most important benefits of positive training is it helps to build a strong bond between you and your dog. The reason for this is positive reinforcement rewards the dog for behaviors you want him to do. Since the dog learns he will benefit by doing what you want, it makes him want to learn. Thus, the dog becomes an active and equal participant in the learning process. Instead of being a robot, your dog is a part of a learning team. Contrast this with a dog whose main concern is avoiding punishment.

Crossing over to positive training methods causes you to look anew at your relationship with your dog. This type of training helps build a co-operative team. Before you can ever think about working with your dog in the show ring, you must have a proper foundation. If you are sensitive to what your dog needs to learn to succeed, he will naturally be more attentive and focused on you, which makes teaching him easier. A dog trained positively wants to work with you. He will want to show for you, too, which will increase his chance of success in the ring.

I see many fractured human-canine relationships where there seems to be little connection and partnership between the dog and the human. The dog seems to be on the end of the lead just along for the ride with the handler paying little or no attention to the dog and what he is doing. It astounds me that these dogs with disconnected handlers ever learn the

The author enjoying life with her dog Hagrid.

skills they need to function well in the show ring. With positive reinforcement training, you have a dog who can cope with showing. You teach your dog in ways that are kind, sound, and make sense to the dog. The dog learns that you reward him for correct behavior, which makes him eager to learn. If your dog doesn't have faith in you, he won't be able to give you his best. To achieve real success in the show ring, the dog has to be able to give it his all.

Building a Foundation

How do you build a positive relationship with your dog? Here are several principles to keep in mind:

1. Treat and view your dog as your partner

2. Nothing in life is free (earning rewards is good)

3. Feeding time is a training opportunity

4. Your dog is not an inanimate object

5. Communication is a two-way street

Treat Your Dog as a Partner!

Good relationships are built on trust, communication and mutual respect. They are never built on fear or intimidation. You must see your dog as a living, breathing partner in order to be a good teacher. You must be willing to teach him and communicate with him in a way he can understand. Think of your dog and yourself as a team or as partners.

Many owners think that a dog should do whatever is asked of him. They believe that with minimal training, the dog should do what the "master" tells him and if he doesn't, the dog is being stubborn or willful. Owners expect behaviors from dogs they do not expect from cats or other animals. In fact, owners often expect more from their dogs than they do from their children, spouses, or friends. Dogs are smart, but they aren't perfect. They are not born knowing what humans want. They have to be trained. They have to be given clear information and and taught in a language they understand. They need to be treated as partners.

Realize that every minute that you spend with your dog is a training opportunity. Dogs are always watching, observing and soaking in what is going on. Taking breaks from teaching does not mean the dog stops learning. Be aware that your actions always impact your dog. Every interaction is an opportunity to strengthen or weaken the relationship and foundation between your dog.

Nothing in Life is Free
To be a good trainer, your dog must understand that you will help guide him in the right direction. He must trust that you will teach him and lead him in a kind, reasonable, and responsible way. The first step is to teach your dog to earn what he wants whenever possible. Teach him that nothing in life is free, but that you will give him what he wants and needs in return for doing what you ask of him.

The idea here is that you will do your part, but he must do his part. His part means that he says, "Please," by sitting (or by doing some other behavior he has been taught) when you ask before he receives dinner, a cookie, or a walk. Don't throw away valuable training opportunities— they are too important. What is valuable to your dog (meals, cookies, and walks) can be used to reinforce behavior. A dog who is asked to earn a living is willing to work with his partner.

Be smart about how you control and give out resources; this is key to an effective partnership. The best way to control behavior is to the control the resources. Find what drives your dog and use it to your advantage.

Here's an example. One of my dogs is obsessed with pine cones. Billy loves it when I kick pine cones on our walks, so I integrated that into training. I kick pine cones, but only after Billy sits, lies down, backs up, spins right or left, or does another behavior he knows. If I pay him with something valuable (a pine cone), he tries harder to do the behaviors that I like, when I ask.

Allowing access to a resource in exchange for good behavior can help build a solid relationship with your dog.

Teaching your dog that he must earn his resources forces you to communicate with him effectively, and will make you a reasonable, calm, sound teacher in the dog's eyes. If you are a good partner and good teacher, training comes easier, and your dog will be attentive and focused, all of which makes him a flashier show dog.

Feeding Time is Training Time

Feed your dog meals rather than free-feeding. Free-feeding means that you leave food available to your dog at all times rather than feeding at a specific and limited time. Free-feeding is flawed for several reasons. First, it is important to know when your dog eats so you can decide the best times for training (not right after a meal). If your dog is permitted to eat whenever he chooses, it makes training more difficult because he may not be hungry. Unlimited access to food also makes it more difficult to control calories when losing or gaining weight is necessary.

Train your dog to follow certain rules at meal times. If he doesn't follow the rules, you can say "Uh-oh," meaning he has not earned what wants. From the time my puppies (show and pet) are very young, they are taught the basic behaviors such as sit and down. To strengthen these behaviors, I will, for example, make their dinner and say, "Sit." If they sit, I say, "Yes" and immediately feed them. If they don't sit, I say, "Uh-oh," withhold dinner, and walk out of the room for a few minutes, then try again. The pups learn that they can have what is important to them, but only when they do what I ask first. This is an incredibly sound and easy way of building a relationship with your dog in which he knows that you are in control, will take care of him, and reward him when he acts appropriately.

Your Dog Is Not an Inanimate Object

Realize your dog is a thinking animal, not an inanimate object that can be forced to do your bidding. Owners are often frustrated and angry because they think a dog takes too long to understand a lesson. However, it isn't fair to be angry at a dog when he doesn't comprehend what you want. Think of it like this: Your native language is English and you take a class to learn French. The language is difficult, and you struggle to understand. The teacher accuses you of being stubborn, willful, or dominant because you don't get it. Is it logical to get into trouble simply because you need clarification? No. Imagine how your dog must feel. Remember that a show or a performance dog must like what he is doing. Frustration, boredom, or confusion is visible, and you don't want to show a dog who isn't having fun or worse or looks as though he is struggling. When your dog is confused or needs clarification, help him! Make sure he knows what you want so he can give you his best.

I recently had the experience of being clicker-trained at a canine behavior group meeting. When I was escorted out of the room so that the group could decide which behaviors to teach me, I felt nervous and uncomfortable. I was afraid I would not get it and would embarrass myself. I actually felt anxious! I knew I would not be hurt physically (they were clicker trainers after all), but I was still anxious. Luckily, the trainer who taught me had great finesse and impeccable timing, and trained me to do several things in a few minutes, such as touch a toy when a specific playing card was face up, and touch a die when a different card was face up. It was a great experience because it forced me to understand how a dog might feel when he is being taught with a clicker. It must be frustrating to be a dog and not be able to say you need more information. I can't imagine how scary it must be when trained with brute force.

Keep in mind that, just like people, dogs sometimes don't feel good, have bad days or are frustrated. Take your dog's mood into account. Dogs aren't people and they probably don't feel emotions like humans, but their attitude on a particular day should be taken into consideration. If the dog resists training, you may have to dig deeper to find out why. Only then can you persuade him to work willingly. Dogs are incredibly honest. They will tell you if they can't perform, when they are scared, or if they are confused or frustrated. Your job is to pay attention, and look for answers.

Communication is a Two-Way Street
Communication is essential to a healthy relationship. You must be able, and willing, to communicate with your dog clearly so he understands what you want and what you are trying to say. Failure to communicate clearly creates frustration for both dog and owner. Positive reinforcement techniques tells the dog, in no uncertain terms, and without emotion, when he does something correctly. Positive training allows him to try behaviors, make mistakes and learn from those mistakes.

It is equally important that an owner understands what his dog is saying. All owners can benefit by learning basic canine body language. You can gain a wealth of knowledge about your dog by understanding what he is saying. While it is beyond the scope of this book to go into a detailed discussion of canine body language, there are several great books on the topic, such as *On Talking Terms with Dogs* and *Canine Body Language* you can read for more information (see Resources).

Most dogs make it clear when they are stressed, relaxed, excited, or frustrated. Owners just need to know what to look for. Recognizing a dog's stress signals is particularly important. Doing so gives you insight into how your dog is feeling and what he is thinking. Body language such as excessive ground sniffing, panting when it isn't hot, holding the tail down, or holding the head down are signs of stress. Learn to recognize your dog's relaxed body language so you know when he stressed and when he is calm and happy.

Keep Working
Training takes time and effort, but remember it is important to keep working on your relationship with your dog. Instructing some dogs is easy, while others are more challenging. As your dog's partner, you owe it to him and yourself to work through difficulties. It can be tough, but I'm

here to tell you that there is not a more rewarding way to live with a dog than when you have a solid relationship and work together as a team.

Chapter 4
POSITIVE TRAINING
FUNDAMENTALS

Training show ring behaviors using positive techniques begins with an understanding of several fundamental concepts. Mastering the following basic concepts will help you become a better trainer and handler.

Learning Theory Basics

Dogs do what works for them. If a dog gets something he wants by exhibiting a certain behavior, he is likely to repeat the behavior. Thus, dogs learn by association and consequences. When a dog learns by association, it is called classical conditioning. An example of classical conditioning is a dog who gets excited when his owner picks up a leash. The dog learns that the leash is always paired with a walk, which the dog enjoys. The dog associates the leash with the walk. The leash "tells" the dog that a walk is upcoming.

When a dog learns by consequences, it is called operant conditioning. The dog learns that he can control his environment with behaviors. Some behaviors cause a pleasant consequence and some behaviors cause an unpleasant consequence.

Operant conditioning has four basic components: positive reinforcement, negative reinforcement, negative punishment, and positive punishment. Positive and negative do not imply good and bad, but a specific meaning in relation to training. Positive means something is given to the dog (think plus). Negative means something is taken away from the dog (think minus).

Here are examples of each. If a dog does something (sits) and his owner gives him a cookie, the dog is likely to repeat the behavior. This is positive reinforcement. Positive reinforcement means that something pleasant happens to the dog following a behavior and because of that pleasant consequence, the behavior is likely to be repeated. People are the same way. You repeat behaviors that are reinforcing or rewarding. You go to work because you receive a paycheck. That paycheck serves as reinforcement to continue working.

Now let's look at it from another angle. You might also be persuaded to work if someone were holding a gun to your head and forcing you. You wouldn't like it as much and it would change your perspective on your job, but you would go to work because there is a gun pointed at your head. This is called negative reinforcement. You have been negatively reinforced for going to work (the scary gun goes away when you agree to go to work), so you go. Both positive (the paycheck) and negative (the gun) reinforcement can cause a behavior to increase in frequency, though positive persuasion is clearly more rewarding and enjoyable than negative. If you make training fun, rewarding and exciting for your dog, he will do whatever you ask. It truly is that simple.

The next component in operant conditioning is negative punishment. Sounds bad, but it isn't. Negative punishment means taking something pleasant away from the dog to inhibit or stop a behavior. A good example of negative punishment is ignoring a dog for jumping up. Dogs often jump up on people because it is reinforcing. The dog receives attention (like petting), which serves to reinforce the behavior. If you cross your arms and turn away, thereby ignoring the jumping, the jumping up will lessen in frequency. You take away something pleasant—your attention—from the dog.

Finally, we come to positive punishment. This is the component of operant conditioning that I do not recommend when training dogs, even though an unwanted behavior may stop. Positive punishment is applying something unpleasant (often painful) to the dog to eliminate a behavior. For example, kneeing a dog in the chest for jumping up, whacking a dog with a newspaper, or jerking the leash. Positive punishment can be as harmless as squirting water from a spray bottle at a barking dog or as painful as leash jerks or electric shocks.

The methods I use are primarily positive reinforcement and, occasionally, negative punishment. I do not use positive punishment and negative reinforcement because while these methods can be effective at first, they are difficult to execute properly, are not usually effective over time, and are not dog friendly. Dogs usually form a negative association with the owner (who doles out the corrections), and to training in general. A dog that receives positive punishment frequently is not a willing and enthusiastic learner. He is likely to avoid both training and his handler in order to avoid being punished in ways that hurt or frighten him.

It is better to reward your dog when he does something right than punish him for doing something wrong. Decide what you would like him to do and then teach and reward him rather than punish what you don't like.

Clicker Training—How it Works

The clicker is a small, box-shaped training tool that makes a "click-click" sound when you press it. (It sounds like a toy metal cricket.) The clicker is used solely as reward marker to indicate to the dog the exact moment he did something correctly and that he will be rewarded for doing it. There is nothing magical about the clicker; the sound it makes simply helps the dog know when he has done something right and his reward is on the way! Nothing more, nothing less. Clicker training isn't difficult, but it is different from other training methods you may have tried. Clicker training is simple, and once you

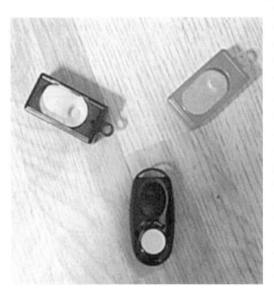

Clickers come in a variety of types and colors. Choose the one that works best for you and your dog.

18

master the basics it is easy to understand and execute complex training tasks with fantastic results.

The "click" is always followed by a reward and, in most cases, the reward is a treat. A reinforcer is the same as a reward; the two words are interchangeable for the purpose of explanation. Food is the strongest reinforcer for most dogs, and it is best if you can find a variety of treats that your dog really likes. The treats should be more valuable than kibble. Many owners say that their dogs are not motivated by food, but the truth is dogs are food-motivated. Food is survival to dogs. If your dog isn't motivated by a particular treat, try something different, such as turkey, hot dogs, or liver treats. Dry kibble or dry biscuits may be rewarding to some dogs, but for most dogs kibble isn't good enough to keep them interested. Train your dog when you know he is hungry. Use different treats. You may be able to use a less tasty treat at home, but you will need a super-delicious reward at shows and competitions where there are distractions. This is normal and perfectly acceptable.

Remember that a click is always followed by a treat. The reward is called a primary reinforcer and the click is what is called a secondary reinforcer. The dog learns to associate the click with food. Think of how your dog acts when you open his treat jar or dog food bag. By itself, the action and sound of opening the jar or bag means nothing, but because it is always followed by a meal, the dog learns to come running when he hears it. In the same way, the clicking sound tells the dog when a reward is coming; therefore, every time you click you must treat. This is an important rule to remember. Even if you make a mistake in timing, it is your job to treat the dog anyway. Failing to do so will cause the clicker to lose power.

Owners sometimes complain that there is too much to handle (leash, clicker, treats), but your reward doesn't have to be in your hand. Place it in your bait bag and grab it after you click. Don't worry if it takes a second to get the treat. You made a promise to the dog by clicking that a treat is coming. He will understand as long as you are consistent.

As you begin clicker training, keep these two, simple rules in mind:

1. Be sure to treat after each click. This is crucial.

2. Click right at the moment the dog does what you like. This may take practice on your part.

Positive training does not require a clicker. However, I have found that the clicker gives me a higher rate of reliability with my dogs because it communicates clearly to the dog and, thereby, makes learning easier.

The clicker is a training tool used primarily to train new behaviors, so you will not have to worry about using the clicker forever or taking it into the ring. Once a behavior is learned, you can use a verbal reward marker in place of the clicker, which is especially useful with show dogs. When choosing a verbal reward marker, make sure it isn't a word that you use frequently in normal conversations because the dog will be confused when you say it and then not reward him. Typical verbal markers are "Yes" or "Click." Try to say it in a tone that is distinct, and always follow up with a treat. The verbal reward marker, of course, is always available and can be used in the ring and in other circumstances where the clicker is not allowed or available.

Some dogs are genuinely afraid or suspicious of the clicker. These dogs usually warm up once they realize that the distinct sound equals food. You can try one of the quiet clickers on the market, or an electronic type that makes different, less snappy sounds. Other options are to use a clicker but muffle the sound by clicking it inside a sweatshirt sleeve or jacket. If you use an extremely tasty reward that the dog finds irresistible, he will adjust to whatever type of clicker you use.

"Charging" the Clicker

One of the first steps is to "charge" your clicker. Charging the clicker means teaching the dog click equals treat. This is very important. You can certainly treat without clicking, but the clicker will lose its power if you don't "pay" the dog for the right behavior after you click. If you are planning on using a verbal reward marker, simply say the word in place of clicking. Everything else is exactly the same.

Step 1. Arm yourself with a clicker and some tasty, fabulous treats. Remember, use a treat that is highly rewarding to the dog.

Step 2. "Click" the clicker and give your dog a treat. Move away and do it again. Repeat this about ten times, making sure that you and your dog are moving around between clicks and treats. The idea is that you click and treat in different positions. You also want to make sure that the dog isn't doing the same behavior each time you click (such as sitting) or he will begin to associate the particular behavior with the click and treat. Move around, click and treat. Vary your timing. Treat immediately, then wait a second or two. Charge the clicker in different rooms of the house. Spend several sessions charging the clicker. You want the dog to learn that a click always means a reward is on the way.

Rodeo is learning that each click means a treat is coming. This is charging the clicker.

Step 3. To make sure your dog is conditioned to the clicker, let him turn away from you and then click. If he immediately turns his head around looking for the treat, you know you have charged the clicker successfully. It isn't necessary to charge the clicker before every training session. Once the clicker is charged, you can move on.

The Behavior You Want

The idea with clicker training is to use the clicker to mark a behavior you want and then reinforce it by giving the dog a treat. How do you first get the behavior to occur? There are three different ways to elicit behavior. All three are valid methods of encouraging behavior, and all these techniques work.

1. **Luring.** Luring means that you use something (usually food) to lure the dog into position or a behavior. Holding a cookie

Murphy is being lured into a sit with a piece of meat.

21

up over a dog's head to encourage him to sit is an example of luring. As the dog sits, you click and treat.

2. **Shaping.** Sometimes referred to as free shaping, this method requires you to begin with movements (or approximations) toward the correct behavior and build from there. You reinforce (click and treat) each step toward a desired behavior. For example, a dog is rewarded as he begins to lower his hips (click and treat), rewarded as his hips hit the ground (click and treat), then rewarded only when he has accomplished a complete sit (click and treat).

3. **Capturing.** With capturing, you reward (click and treat) your dog when he does the desired behavior on his own, with no prompting from you. You simply wait for the dog to sit and then reward (click and treat). This method takes longer, but once a behavior is captured the dog is quick to learn it will earn him a reward.

Placing a Behavior on Cue

Once the dog has accomplished a behavior, it must be placed on cue. A cue is simply a verbal command. Waiting for the dog to accomplish the behavior before adding a cue may seem counterintuitive, but you must be sure the dog clearly understands the behavior. Next, you teach the dog to associate a word ("sit," for instance) with the behavior the dog is doing (sitting). This concept can be frustrating to owners who want to say the word to the dog right away, but it is truly better to wait until the behavior is learned. After all, dogs do not understand words. They can learn to understand consequences. Once a behavior is learned, then add a verbal command. Remember that until the dog associates the command with the behavior, the word is a meaningless. If you say the command over and over before the dog understands, you are not training the dog to associate the word with the behavior, you are teaching him to ignore what you are saying.

Knowing when to add the cue is simple. Add the cue as soon as the dog offers the behavior. For example, if you are trying to teach your dog to gait, use whatever command you choose when the dog finds the proper position and follow up the cue immediately with a click and treat.

Once the dog has learned a behavior and is rewarded for doing it, the dog will offer the behavior. This is key because a dog who offers behaviors to get rewards is a dog who is excited about learning. Offering a behavior means that the dog will try a behavior on his own for a reward. He will sit, lie down, walk next to you and do whatever has been reinforced in the past to earn rewards.

You do not need to reward your dog every time he offers a behavior. If you are teaching "sit," and the dog repeatedly lies down, you simply ignore the incorrect behavior he offers. You are not required to run frantically looking for the clicker and treats because your dog offers a behavior. Give verbal praise for offering behaviors at appropriate times if you aren't armed with a clicker or treats. You choose the training sessions, not the dog!

More Positive Training Techniques and Terminology

Once your dog offers behaviors and is rewarded accordingly, you can try a few advanced training techniques. These techniques are discussed in greater detail in Chapters 6 through 8. Briefly, these techniques include: generalizing; varying rewards and reinforcement schedules; raising criteria and building duration; the no-reward marker; chaining; and fading the use of the clicker

Generalizing

Once a behavior is learned and placed on command, you can use the clicker to generalize the behavior to new locations and with new distractions. Generalizing means the behavior is reliable in different locations with a variety of distractions. This is critical, of course, for a show dog. You may have trained your dog to stack perfectly at home, but if he won't do it in the show ring you have not accomplished what you want. It is critical to train behaviors in a variety of locations and with a variety of distractions.

It is important to understand that most dogs don't generalize well. This means that you must train in different locations. If you only train in your kitchen, with no distractions, the dog will be unreliable when there are new, more challenging distractions nearby.

Varying Rewards and Reinforcement Schedules

Once a behavior is learned, on command and reliable, you can reward your dog with verbal and physical praise, toys, belly rubs and treats. Whatever your dog likes eventually becomes the reward. Food is a very powerful reward, but it is not necessary to use it all the time.

You do not need to use the clicker (or whatever reward marker you are using) every time your dog performs a behavior correctly. This is called variable reinforcement. Variable reinforcement means you reward less and randomly, but still reward. In essence, you keep the dog guessing when he will receive a reward.

When you teach new behaviors to your dog, reinforce and reward for every "right" answer. Once the behavior is solid and on cue, you can click and treat every two or three times. Continue to reward the dog throughout his life, using anything he likes such as a belly rub or a game of tossing the ball. Remember, you wouldn't work for just a pat on the back and neither will your dog. "Payment" is necessary some of the time.

Raising Criteria and Building Duration
Raising criteria is adding challenges or increased levels of difficulty to a behavior. For example, at first you click when your dog walks next to you. Then you click when he walks next to you with his head up. Adding criteria means asking for a bit more before clicking. A common way to raise criteria is to ask the dog to perform a behavior over a longer period of time before rewarding. This is known as building duration. For example, you click and treat when the dog sits for five seconds. Over time, you build the duration of sitting to one minute or more.

No-Reward Marker
At some point in your training, you may use what is called a no-reward marker. Just as the click tells the dog he did a behavior correctly and a treat is coming, the no-reward marker (NRM) tells the dog, "Try again. You didn't earn a reward." You can use the word, "Oops," "Wrong" or "Too bad." Don't say the word in a harsh or stern voice. It is not a verbal reprimand, but information to the dog. A NRM is usually not used at the beginning stages of training. The absence of a click is usually sufficient to tell the dog he needs to try again, and it may frustrate him to use a NRM. However, once behaviors are learned, the no-reward marker can be helpful.

Chaining
There comes a time when you ask the dog to do several behaviors in succession. This is called chaining. For example, teaching the dog to move down and back, and then stop and free stack in the show ring is chaining several behaviors together. When you train a sequence, you have to first break down each behavior: teach the free stack, teach proper move-

ment, teach the turn. Once each behavior is solid and on cue, put them together.

Fading the Clicker

The clicker is used primarily when teaching new behaviors, and to generalize behaviors. Once your dog knows the commands and is performing reliably, you will not have to click every time the dog does a desired behavior correctly. You can begin to fade or reduce its use. So don't worry about not being able to take the clicker into the ring, because your dog will learn to perform behaviors without the need for a the clicker. Once the behaviors are learned and on command, continue to reward some of the time with food or toys the dog enjoys.

Helpful Hints

Keep your training sessions short, between two and three minutes. Training during television commercials works well. Don't think a training session has to be a big deal; it doesn't. Keep treats and a clicker in your kitchen and train for a few minutes when you go to the refrigerator to get a drink.

You can teach several new behaviors concurrently, but each behavior should be taught during a different training session. In other words don't work on two behaviors together until each behavior has been learned and placed on cue separately.

Getting Ready for the Show Ring

Now that you know positive training theory and techniques, you can teach your dog the skills he needs to succeed in the show ring. There are three foundation behaviors every a show dog needs to master:

1. Gait or move on leash so that the judge can view the dog's movement.

2. Stack or stand still so the judge can see the dog's profile when standing.

3. Stand still for examination by the judge.

Once you have the proper equipment (see Chapter 5), you can take what you have learned here to start training show ring behaviors. Okay, ready to head to the show ring? Start clicking!

Chapter 5
EQUIPMENT

When you walk into a pet supply store or a vendor booth at a dog show, the amount of equipment available is overwhelming. There are buckle collars, martingale or limited slip collars, slip collars, collars made of leather, fabric and chain, and prong collars; leads of every style and length, made of fabric and leather, retractable leads, thirty foot leads; all-in-one collars (collar and leash attached), head halters and harnesses. The list goes on and on. No need for confusion, though. The following is a simple list of equipment I recommend for positively training show dogs.

A Minimalist Approach

Show dog equipment should be minimal. The equipment (and you) should fade into the background, and only the dog should shine. Equipment should closely match the color of the dog. Do not choose neon or bright colors, such as hot pink or orange even if they are your favorite colors. It diverts attention away from the dog. Flashy or bright colors are fine for everyday collars, but you want the judge to focus on the dog, not the equipment. (I remember a breeder said that some owners like to use a blue lead so the judge will think of the blue ribbon. I don't think so! You aren't going to fool a judge into giving your dog a first place because the lead was blue and if you did, I would question the integrity of that judge.)

There is much worry about equipment to make a dog do this or that. If you build a good relationship with your dog, and take time to train, you don't have to worry about equipment. The dog is willing to do what you ask and will do it "naked." A lead and collar is considered safety equipment, designed to keep the dog safe and connected to you. If you need special collars or leads to gain control of the dog, then the dog needs more training. Do not get in the habit of relying on specialized equipment to train or show dogs. That approach will eventually backfire because at some point the dog will not respond to the equipment.

Choke Chains/Slip Collars

The most common collar seen at dog shows is the choke chain or slip collar. Choke chains come in chain, fabric and leather. This is the traditional chain collar that is a simple chain with a ring at both ends. The chain is slipped through one ring and it makes a collar. Slip collars have been used for years, though just because they has been around a long time, doesn't mean they are the best choice. The choke chain works by tightening around the neck when a dog resists or pulls. In theory, when he feels the tightening of the collar on his neck, he stops pulling. Some owners insist it is the "sound" of the chain that is intended to change the dog's behavior, but having seen hundreds of dogs wear choke chains, I can tell you that the sound of the chain does nothing. Also, dogs who are touch insensitive (meaning they are hardwired to ignore discomfort), are oblivious to these collars. I have witnessed Rottweilers and Boxers pass out from wearing slip collars.

The choke or slip collar will close up as long as there is any tension.

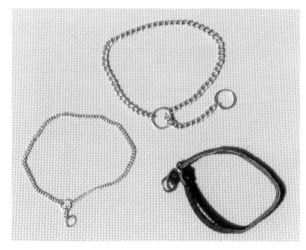

A well-trained show dog does not require a choke chain, and there are better choices besides a collar that chokes. The only "slip" type equipment I use on my dogs is a thick, fleece slip lead (commonly used in agility because they come off quickly) and I only use that on a dog that is trained and doesn't pull on the lead. A dog who has been trained to walk on a loose leash without pulling has a much easier time on a choke chain, although I still don't recommend them. Keep in mind that if a dog is frightened, insecure, confused or frustrated, the added anxiety of a collar that hurts him or cuts off his air will only make matters worse.

Martingale/Limited Slip Collars

Martingale collars are available in different fabrics and materials.

Rodeo is wearing his everyday martingale collar.

A martingale or limited slip collar (sometimes called a greyhound collar) has a second piece of chain or fabric on the collar so that it cannot continue to tighten like a choke collar. This is my first choice for most medium to large-size dogs, and for dogs who are not yet comfortable at dog shows and may attempt to pull away. The limited slip closes just enough so the dog can't pull his head out, but it doesn't continue to tighten. I also recommend martingale collars in my beginning obedience/manners classes. Martingale collars are dog-friendly, and come in a variety of fabrics and materials. Chain martingales are slightly more difficult to find, though they can be found online and at dog shows.

All-In-Ones

There are a variety of all-in-ones, which is a collar and lead connected together. The collar portion of the lead is usually a slip or choke collar, martingale or limited slip collar, or a simple noose type collar. I use the all-in-one Resco™ leads for small show dogs. These are great for dogs who are not likely to slip out of their collar. I prefer Resco because a clip allows you to keep the lead in place on the dog's neck, but it doesn't tighten on the neck. If you have a dog that backs out of his collar, a martingale all-in-one lead is a good choice. When properly fitted, the martingale will close just enough to prevent the dog from pulling his head out. The martingale leads are available in canvas, and chain and nylon. All are accept-

Lester is wearing a Resco all-in-one lead.

Lola is wearing a martingale, all-in-one show lead.

able, though you need to try a few to see what works best. I do not recommend an all-in-one with a slip collar.

Leads

Just like collars, there are many different leads available on the market. Leads, or leashes, are available in leather, nylon, cotton and other materials. I prefer a leather lead. A well-made leather lead is durable—unless a chewer gets it! Leather molds to your hand and is comfortable to hold. For a really small dog, a nylon lead is good because there isn't much pull to cause discomfort. I prefer to use an all-in-one noose or martingale lead with small dogs and a martingale with a very thin leather lead with large dogs. It is especially important to have a comfortable lead that is easy to hold with large breeds.

Bait Bags

A bait bag that offers quick access to treats is essential when you are training. You can use a bait bag in the ring as well, although your "ring bag" should probably be smaller and less obvious. The training bag should be designed so it is easy to reach for treats. The show bag should be small and blend in with your clothing. Of course, if you wear an outfit with pockets, you don't have to worry about a bait bag in the ring.

Practice and training bags on the left and a show treat bag on the right.

Clickers

The once plain, rectangular clicker is now available in a wide range of sizes, styles and sounds. I prefer the "I-click," which is slightly quieter than the standard box clicker. There are also electronic clickers with a range of sounds. Remember that sound is information to the dog, so if you go from a box clicker to an electronic clicker, you will need to retrain. Choose what you want, and keep a few clickers on hand (and treats) so you are constantly armed and ready to train.

Clickers are easy to locate. Most pet supply stores stock them, as well as dog show vendors and online suppliers. If you have trouble finding clickers, check out the Resources section.

Bait

Bait depends on the individual dog. A dog who needs higher motivation in the ring needs higher value rewards. Of course, the value of the reward depends on the individual dog, but some good choices are cheese, hot dogs and cooked liver. A dog who is easy-going and motivated by food will work for less than a dog who isn't motivated by food. Evaluate the individual dog to determine the best bait of choice.

Equipment Recommendations
Leads and Collars:

1. For small dogs who don't pull out of their collars: Resco lead with noose at the end.

2. For small dogs who do pull of their collars: Martingale All-In-One.

3. Medium dogs: Martingale All-In-One or a Martingale with a light lead attached.

4. Large dogs: Martingale collar with leather lead attached.

Clickers: I-Click quiet clicker.

Practice Bait Bag: Premier™ treat bag.

Chapter 6
TRAINING YOUR DOG TO GAIT

Gait is one of the most important characteristics by which a conformation judge evaluates your dog. The judge wants to know if the dog moves properly, as defined by its breed standard. For some judges, gait is the single most important aspect of judging a dog because a faulty gait can indicate weakness in the dog's structure.

When a dog moves properly and is shown correctly, it is a beautiful sight; movement is fluid and easy. A mediocre handler can make a nice dog look terrible by holding the lead too tight, moving at an uneven pace, or stopping short. An experienced handler can minimize a dog's flaws by the way he presents the dog to the judge. It is the handler's job to make the dog shine, and training your dog to gait will help him shine brightly.

The goal in training your dog to gait is to teach him to how to move out confidently, slightly in front of you on a loose leash, and then fall back into a comfortable trot. His movement on leash should look fluid and easy and he should cover ground effortlessly. Professional handlers make it look so easy. It is easy, if the dog is well trained. If the dog does not gait well, showing is a frustrating experience for dog and handler.

The dog must know how to properly move in the ring.

Begin Off Lead

Pulling on the lead is a common problem with show dogs. Scents, noise, people and dogs milling about are some of the distractions that cause dogs to pull on the lead. I recommend that handlers begin gait training their dogs off lead to avoid learning the bad habit of pulling. New clients are sometimes wary of off-lead training—until they try it. Off-lead training helps build a relationship with your dog because he learns to work with you, without pressure or discomfort from a leash.

Train in an enclosed area with few distractions—no people, dogs or a blaring television. Make sure there is plenty of room to move around. You'll be training in frequent, short sessions so make the location convenient to you: a large living room, basement, or yard.

Clicker training is a straightforward way to teach gaiting to dogs of any age and size. Using a clicker and treats will keep your dog's focus on you because he is anticipating a reward, and he is less likely to be distracted. Be sure you've thoroughly charged the clicker as discussed in Chapter 4 so your dog knows how the training game works.

Teaching the Proper Gait

Step 1. Place some super-delicious treats in your left hand and let the dog smell the them in your closed hand. This will entice him to focus his attention to your left side. Wait for your dog to look at you, then click and treat to let him know you appreciate his attention.

Lola is learning to move properly with no leash. Note how I hold the food in my left hand.

Step 2. Next, walk around, still holding treats in your left hand. Whenever your dog moves with you, on your left side, click and treat. Do this four to five times a day, in two minute sessions, so your dog understands that when he moves along with you on your left side he is rewarded. Practice this step for a few days until the dog understands what you want. Don't worry if the dog jumps around or moves improperly; as long as he is on your left side, within arm's reach while you are moving, it's okay. Your goal at this stage is to teach him to be at your left side. Once he darts into position when you move, you're ready to move on to Step 3.

Positive Training Tip

Ask an observant friend with good clicker skills to assist you. The assistant can click for correct position as you and your dog move, while you dispense the treats. It is sometimes easier to see correct movement from a distance. An assistant also adds a new element to the training—a new person who acts as a distraction.

Step 3. Repeat Step 2 with one change. Place your treats in a bait bag, not your hand, with the clicker in your right hand. Continue to walk around, and click and treat when your dog is in the correct position. Don't worry about how your dog moves. Repeat this until your dog automatically moves into a left-side position when you begin walking. Then move on to Step 4.

Step 4. When the dog is reliably moving into position as you walk, it's time to work on how the dog is moving. With treats in your bait bag and a clicker in your right hand, walk around. Watch how your dog moves. Your goal is to click and treat only when he moves properly (no skipping, pacing, or hopping). Click and treat frequently when he moves correctly so he understands what you want. If your dog moves incorrectly sometimes, it's no problem. Just do not click and treat.

Adding the Lead

For a puppy or dog who is not comfortable with a lead, attach the lead and let him drag it around. Always hold the lead in your left hand. Practice rolling up the lead in your hand so you can avoid draping it over your dog, which can be distracting to the judge. Work on the gaiting exercises in the previous section with the lead attached. Once the dog appears comfortable with the lead, move on to the training steps outlined below.

Cap'n Jack is learning how to accept a leash by walking around with it hanging behind him while he gets enticed with a treat.

On-Lead Training

Step 1. Attach the show lead to your dog. Put some yummy treats in your bait bag, not in your hand. Hold the clicker in your right hand and the lead in your left hand. Take a step forward and click and treat if the dog takes off with you. Continue to click and treat often if your dog walks alongside you. If he pulls on the lead, stop walking, say, "Uh-oh," and go back to where you started. The dog must learn that pulling doesn't get him where he wants to go—ahead.

🐕
Positive Training Tip

I prefer to show a dog on a loose lead so the judge can really see his movement. In fact, walking on a loose lead is a requirement when showing some breeds. If a dog is straining against the lead, it is not only uncomfortable for him, but it doesn't show true movement. Reward only loose-leash walking. Teaching the dog not to pull and to walk at the speed you want, looks more natural and is more appealing to a judge.

🐕
Positive Training Tip

Do not jerk the leash if the dog pulls, or moves too fast. Simply stop moving forward and go back to where you started. A dog pulls on the leash because he has previously been reinforced. In other words, the dog pulls and receives what he wants. Your goal is to take the reward out of pulling.

Step 2. Next, move around at the pace you want the dog to move in the show ring. When he moves properly, click and treat, often. If you reinforce often, the dog is likely to repeat the behavior. Practice this at least once a day (two or three times is better), a few minutes each session, for a week. Very quickly you have a dog that moves properly.

Step 3. Once the dog is in the correct position and moves at a good speed, you can teach a cue. Say, "Let's go" (or whatever cue you want), as the dog assumes position just before you click and treat. Practice this in several short training sessions. This is the sequence:

1. Take off walking; the dog moves correctly.

2. You say, "Let's go."

3. Click and treat.

4. Repeat.

This is how to cue a behavior. You first want the dog to know the behavior so that when you use a verbal cue the dog knows exactly with what to associate that word.

Step 4. Say, "Let's go," just before you take off. Click and treat if the dog takes off with you, and periodically click and treat as he does it correctly.

Step 5. Once your dog knows how to gait on cue, you can practice the behavior at new, more distracting locations.

Step 6. If you practice gaiting with your dog at home and at other locations, he should be fairly reliable. Stop using the clicker and vary the rewards. Use treats, then verbal and physical praise, or favorite toys. It is essential that you continue to reward the dog periodically or you may discourage the behavior you have worked so hard to train. Vary the reward, but continue to reward.

Cowboy has learned to move well on leash as well as off leash.

Touch

Touch is a behavior that is very helpful in teaching a dog to gait, and can help teach other show dog skills. If the dog is taught the command, "Touch," and will touch his nose to where you direct him, you can use this behavior to improve movement and positioning. Touch is an example of what trainers call "targeting," a behavior that can be used in a number of training applications.

You can use the "Touch" command many ways in the show ring. It can be used with dogs

H
Positive Training Tip

If you trained your dog with a verbal marker such as, "Yes" or "Click," you can say those phrases to let him know when he is performing correctly. Also, remember that dogs have difficulty generalizing, so reward the dog in and out of the show ring. If you attend a conformation training class, talk to your instructor about using the clicker in class. This will help the dog generalize the behaviors to new locations.

that put their noses to the ground or with dogs that lag behind or with dogs who pull on the lead. Beyond gaiting, touch can be helpful for overcoming fear because dogs who are fearful will perform a touch when asked.

Teaching the Touch

Begin by asking the dog to touch either your hand or an object, such as a touch stick, with his nose. Your hand or the stick can serve as the "target." You can purchase a touch stick (see Resources) or you can make one with a wooden dowel (1/2-inch thick, 2 feet in length). Wrap a piece of colored tape around one end or paint it so that there is about 2 inches of color on one end of the stick. This makes it easier for the dog to see. Yellow is a good color choice. Once you have a touch stick you are ready to begin.

Step 1. With the touch stick in one hand and the clicker in the other, place the colored end of the stick in front of the dog's nose, about an inch away. (If you choose to use your hand, simply replace the touch stick with your hand.) A naturally curious dog will lean forward to see why the stick or your hand is so close to his face. As soon as he leans forward and touches it with his nose, click and treat. It is important that you keep the target very close at first. You want the dog to succeed.

Billy learning to follow a touch stick.

If your dog doesn't touch the target in the first session, click and treat him for looking toward the target. In the next session, do not click when he looks at it, which will encourage him to move toward it. Click movement toward the stick. Continue in this way until the dog touches the target. This is an example of shaping behavior as discussed in Chapter 4

Step 2. After several sessions, the dog should move forward as soon as he sees the target (this is a very easy way to earn a reward, after all). You can say, "Touch," as soon as he touches the target. This is the sequence:

1. Present the target and the dog touches it with his nose.

2. You say, "Touch," as he touches the target, then click and treat.

3. Say, "Touch," when the dog touches the target for a few days.

4. Next, present the target and say, "Touch." The dog associates touching the target with his nose and the command, "Touch." Now the behavior is on cue. If not, go back to Step 1 and work on shaping the touch.

Once the dog touches the target consistently, ask him to touch the target as you move it a few inches away. Continue to raise the criteria by gradually increasing the distance.

A dog that follows a target reliably can easily learn to gait because the target lures him as he moves. Targeting also teaches a dog to keep his head up, a must for the show ring.

Chapter 7

TEACHING A DOG TO STACK

Stacking means the dog stands still in a show position or show stance. Free-stacking means the dog stacks without any help from his handler; he learns how to set himself up. Whether you help the dog or not, a stacked dog is considered properly set up when his front legs are placed directly under his front assembly and his rear legs are set correctly. Knowing how to stack is incredibly important. A handsome dog stacked incorrectly looks mediocre; a good dog stacked correctly looks great. You should know how to set up your dog properly, and your dog should be able to perform a free-stack on cue.

Hampton has learned to hold a nice stack on the table for the approaching judge.

How a dog is stacked for examination is based on individual breed standards. Details for specific breeds are beyond the scope of this book. Check your dog's breed standard to learn more, and attend dog shows to watch professional handlers stack dogs for the judge. You can also contact your national breed club for resources, such as recordings of specialty shows. A video recording provides an opportunity to view many dogs of your particular breed to get a solid picture of a proper stack.

Practice stacking in front of a mirror. A dog can look very different from a distance than right in front of you. Standing over and looking down at the dog gives a different view than looking at the dog a few feet away. Setting up the dog in front of a mirror helps you see what the judge sees from across the ring.

Use the clicker to teach free-stacking. This method gives clear information to the dog, and makes it easy for him to succeed. Whether a dog can free-stack determine if he wins. Obviously, it is much easier for a judge to look at a dog who is standing rock solid rather than wiggling around. Also, a great free-stacker is flashy to watch. He looks like he's demanding the win!

Teaching a dog to stack is easy at first and gradually becomes more challenging. The dog learns to how to stand, then progresses to standing on cue, and standing correctly. Then how to move, stop, and perform a free stack.

This puppy is learning to hold a free-stack while being touched by both handler and judge..

Stand On the Ground

These instructions will show you how to teach your dog to free-stack. However, you may need to reposition your dog's legs at times. This is okay. Most importantly, you must be able to stack your dog quickly and easily, and he must hold the position during examination.

Begin by teaching your dog to stand on the ground. Don't be concerned at this point about how the dog is standing or positioned. You just want the dog to stand and feel comfortable. Start inside your home, with no distractions. If you need more room you can train outside, but keep distractions to a minimum.

Step 1. Place a clicker and treats in your right hand. The dog can be on lead or off, but I prefer to start off lead if you are working in a secure area.

Step 2. Simply click and treat when your dog stands. It doesn't matter if he is standing crooked or square, right or wrong. Just be sure he is standing. Stand is an interesting skill to teach because at first the dog looks at you wondering what he did to deserve a reward. If he continues standing, click and treat again. For a few sessions or a few days, depending on your dog, click and treat whenever he stands. Eventually, the dog will "offer" stands to see if you click. Once the dog offers stands on his own, work on the stand with a lead attached.

If the dog doesn't stand readily on his own, lure him into the standing position with a treat. Place the treat in front of his nose and move it forward. As soon as he stands, click and treat. The goal is to capture stands

with the clicker as they occur, and to lure him into position with treats. To be successful in the show ring, it helps to have experience with both techniques.

Rodeo is clicked and treated just for standing.

Cowboy being lured with a treat from a sit into a stand.

Step 3. Once the dog offers a stand, place it on cue by saying, "Stand," right after he stands and before you click and treat. Do this for several days until the dog associates the cue ("Stand") with the behavior of standing.

Step 4. Next, test to see if your dog can reliably perform a stand. Ask your dog to "Stand." There is a good chance, at this point, that the dog may sit instead. To help him along, right after you say the cue, step toward your dog, which will cause him to stand up. Click and treat immediately. Practice this for a few days, and he should improve.

It is okay to lure the stand, and to click and treat multiple times if the dog continues to stand. This teaches the dog to stand and stay in place.

Kaeli is clicked for standing when I ask her to "Stand."

Step 5. Once the dog understands the stand command and is comfortable standing, continue to practice regularly.

Teaching the Stand-Stay

After the dog has learned to stand comfortably, you will teach him to stay in the stand position. When you are showing, your dog will need to hold the stand while he is examined by the judge and during the class lineup. Work on building duration up to a minute or two. Keep in mind that you can talk to your dog while he is being examined by the judge. Also, let the dog relax part of the time in the ring if the judge is not looking at him. If you are standing in a class of twelve dogs, you can't expect your dog to hold a stack while the other eleven are being judged. Just be sure the dog is stacked when the judge looks at him. Finally, don't allow your dog to showcase his weaknesses to the judge while waiting in line, just in case the judge glances down the line. For instance, if your dog has a faulty rear, don't allow him to stand relaxed with his rear to the judge.

Step 1. Ask the dog to stand either by giving a verbal cue or by stepping forward to encourage him to stand. As soon as he stands, click and treat. If he remains standing, click and treat again immediately. If your dog sits, say, "Uh-oh" (or whatever your preferred no-reward marker is), and stand him up again. He will quickly learn that "Uh-oh" means he didn't earn a reward and will try again.

Cleo's owner has asked her to stand and then asked her to stay briefly before rewarding her.

Step 2. Ask the dog to stand, and when he stands say, "Good stand." Wait a second or two before clicking and treating. Build the duration of this behavior, from one or two seconds to five seconds, between when he stands and when you click and treat. Switch around when you click and treat, sometimes after three seconds, then five seconds, then one second, and so on.

Step 3. Continue to build duration until your dog can hold the stand for as long as you need him to hold a stand in the show ring. If he sits down or begins to wander, simply say, "Uh-oh," stand him up and start over. Your dog will soon understand that the way to earn a reward is to hold the stand until you click and treat. With regular practice, the dog will have a nice, reliable free-stack. Once he performs the behavior consistently, vary the rewards: treats, a toy or praise.

Specific Body Parts

Once the dog knows how to stand on command, you can work on perfecting the stand-stay, which may include breaking down lessons into specific body parts. The easiest way to teach a dog to "fix" a specific body part is to focus on that part of the body, such as ears, tail, feet or head, during a training session. If, for example, you want to teach your dog to fix his rear end when he stacks, you would follow this formula:

Step 1. Arm yourself with treats and a clicker. Use a food reward that you know your dog cannot resist.

Step 2. In a quiet, distraction-free room, wait for your dog to move his rear end. Click and treat any movement of the hindquarters. This informs the dog who you want something to do with of the rear end of his body. Click and treat the dog several times for rear movement.

Step 3. Next, click and treat only when the dog moves his rear correctly. If he doesn't get it correct right away, he will probably move in a different way in an attempt to get it right. Be ready!

If you are asking the dog to step forward to even out his back legs, you can step into him and away; this "body pressure" will encourage him to find the proper positioning. (Body pressure is using your body to manipulate the space between the dog and you to encourage movement. While not normally thought of as a positive training technique, body pressure functions like a lure.) Click and treat when he gets it right.

If you are trying to fix the placement of a single rear leg, use your body pressure to encourage the dog to move that leg. For example, if you want the dog to move his right rear leg backward, step in slightly with your right foot and right shoulder.

Step 4. Once the dog straightens his rear on his own and is in proper position, put it on command. Tell the dog what you want while he is doing it. (I say to my dogs, "Fix your rear," and they shift around until they are standing square.)

Lola goes from a sitting position to a standing position when I move toward her. Note this is different from the lure where I used food to encourage movement. This was done strictly with my body movement.

Keep in mind that you can always use body pressure to step into or away from the dog to encourage movement toward or away from you. This is when showing a dog turns into an art form. Dogs are creatures of body language. Dogs respond to how their owners move and what their bodies say, more than what their voices say. Think of ground stacking as a dance. If you want the dog to fix his right rear leg, move your right foot and shoulder toward the dog to encourage movement of his opposite rear leg. If you want him to move both rear legs, step gently forward toward the middle of his front legs to encourage him to step back and readjust.

At first, you may have to step toward the dog to encourage him to stand up. Click and treat immediately when he stands, and say, "Uh-oh" (a no-reward marker), and step in again if he sits. It doesn't take long for the dog to figure out what earns a reward. Practice this technique often and you will be amazed at how responsive the dog is to you. Eventually, body pressure, along with a verbal cue such as, "Fix your rear," will teach the dog to readjust his rear because he knows a reward is coming.

It is fine to teach different behaviors concurrently, but each new behavior should be taught in a separate training session. For instance, work on gaiting, take a short break, then work on stacking. When you end that session, play a bit, and move on to something else.

A Word About Bait

Bait is a favorite tool of many handlers to help teach a show dog to hold a stack. Many handlers use bait in the ring for this purpose and I have found that using food in the ring seems to help my dogs enjoy showing more. But whether you will need to or not depends on the individual dog and the training methods you use. For example, with one dog I may want to use it when he is on the table, but with another dog I may only use it when he is in the lineup.

If your dog is not highly motivated by food, you may be able to train him to target your hand or watch your finger instead (see below). But if your dog can be motivated easily to learn by using liver or chicken, bait can be a very effective tool in and out of the ring.

Watch the Finger
Teaching a dog to "Watch the finger" can be helpful when you want the dog to stand still and focus. It can also be helpful for dogs that are highly food-motivated and lose their minds when bait is nearby. Teaching this behavior is simple. It only takes a few sessions for the dog to understand, as long as your timing is good.

Step 1. Begin with your dog on or off leash. Place treats in your bait bag, not in your hand. Place the clicker (and leash if you are using one) in your left hand, and nothing in your right hand.

Step 2. Extend your finger in front of your dog and say nothing.

Step 3. As soon as the dog looks at your finger, click and treat. Repeat this until the dog looks at your finger immediately.

Katie teaches Murphy to watch her finger.

Rex has learned to watch his owner's finger when he stands as if for examination.

Step 4: Once the dog quickly looks at your finger, say, "Watch," or whatever cue you want to use. Immediately click and treat. Practice this for several sessions until the dog will focus on your finger when you say, "Watch."

Step 5. Next, pause a second (just a second) before you click and treat. Once the dog can easily watch your finger for a second, wait a few seconds before you click and treat. Take your time on this. Once the dog watches your finger for a few seconds, vary the reinforcement schedule (four seconds, two seconds, six seconds) to build duration. If the dog continually looks away from the finger, you are moving too fast.

Table Stacking

Table training is essential for small breeds. Be aware that teaching a dog to stack on a table offers additional challenges. However, showing a dog on a table can be an advantage because the dog usually doesn't move around as much as a dog on the ground. For best results, begin table training during puppyhood. If the dog has a positive impression of a table, it makes training for the show easier. If you have a dog who is afraid of the table, read Chapter 9. For dogs who are not afraid, but need table training, read on.

Table Training

Step 1. Be sure bait is readily available, either in your right hand, in your mouth, or in your bait bag. Right before I pick up a dog to place him on the table, I throw the lead over my shoulder or around my neck. I do this to keep it out of the way while I stack the dog; it also keeps the lead high. Do whatever is comfortable for you, but make sure the lead is out of the way.

Katie teaches Murphy to stand on a park table.

Step 2. To pick up your dog, wrap your left forearm over his back and lift him with the left hand under his body. I like to place the dog on the table so he drops his own front true. This means that when I lift him, I lift with my left arm around his body and my right hand goes under his jaw so that when I place him on the table I can gently position his front legs right where they belong. This eliminates the need to reposition his front feet.

Lift your dog onto the table by picking him up securely underneath his body.

Step 3. Place the dog on the table with his front feet fairly close to the edge. By doing this you limit his forward movement on the table. If he can't step forward, then you only need to think about the hindquarters.

Positive Training Tip

When using your hands to position a dog, large or small, be gentle. Many dogs are wiggly and nervous due to a novice handler's rough handling. Your touch should be calming to the dog, not upsetting. If you move a front leg, slide your hand over the dog's body and down the shoulder to the elbow. Move the leg from the elbow. If you have to position the rear legs, slide your hand down the dog's body to each rear leg and reposition carefully. Do not lift up the entire hindquarters and drop it down; this is uncomfortable for most dogs, and they will pull their body weight back making the forequarters unattractive.

Step 4. Once the dog's front end is on the table, move the bait to his mouth so he can nibble on it as you position his rear. When positioning feet, move the front feet gently from the elbow and move the rear legs gently by the hock. Do not grab or jerk the legs.

You won't need a clicker when positioning the dog on the table. Use bait to keep him occu-

Here I use food to keep Lola occupied while I position her legs.

pied while you set him up.

Positive Training Tip

Whatever you do, please do not pretend to drop a dog off the end of the table. This is a nasty, table-training technique. It does nothing but teach a dog to distrust you. It is totally unnecessary.

Step 5. Continue to let the dog nibble on the bait while telling him, "Stay." Practice this until you can set up the dog quickly. At this point, he should remain still.

Step 6. Depending on your dog, there are a few ways to proceed. If your dog is set up and doesn't move, say, "Yes," and give him a treat. If you have taught finger targeting, have him watch your finger. I choose not to use the clicker because I need my hands, and I don't want the dog to think that a click is an invitation to jump or move. Continue practicing until the dog remains standing.

If the dog is wiggly without bait, try this technique instead of the previous one. Place the dog on the table and set him up. Use bait to keep him still while you position him. Once he is set up say, "Stay," and take away the food for a second. If he stays, say, "Yes," and give him the treat. Consider the value of the reward. Don't use a high-value reward because you don't want him to jump forward. Use food that doesn't make him go crazy. Once he can hold a stay with the food in front of him for several seconds, ask him to watch your finger.

Step 7. Place your finger in front of him, and give him the "Stay" cue. If he can stay for a couple of seconds, say, "Yes," and give him a treat from the bait bag. Practice this until he can watch your hand and remain standing still.

Step 8. Once the dog will stay reliably on the table, you can add distractions. Stack him on the table, say, "Stay," and ask a friend to walk up to him. If the dog wiggles and is excited, ask the friend to walk away. Do not give a treat. The consequence for wiggling is the person goes away and no treat. It isn't necessary to jerk, pinch or pull. The dog just needs to know that if he doesn't stay, he doesn't receive a reward. If he does stay, say, "Yes," and give him a treat.

Ground Stacking Large Breeds

Teaching large breeds to stack is similar to teaching the table stack. Teach the dog to hold a free-stack. If he is able to perform an excellent free-stack, you won't need to place your hands on the dog when he is in line. The better the dog can free-stack, the better he will look to the judge.

If you must adjust a large dog when he is on the ground, keep these tips in mind. Gently lift the leg from the elbow, not from the foot. Grabbing the feet is uncomfortable for the dog. Move the back legs by gently taking hold of the leg at the hock joint.

Rather than grabbing at the dog's feet, move his front legs from the elbow.

Remember to move the back legs at the hock.

Always slide your hands over the body so the dog is expecting you to reposition his body. Jerky or rough handling will make the dog wiggly and uncomfortable.

Some dogs are not comfortable when you lean over them; this can be intensified in the ring. For these dogs, move the back legs from underneath rather than over him.

Step 1. Position your dog so he is standing in front of you. Try to walk him into the stack so that his front legs are positioned properly. That way, you only need to reposition the back legs.

Dora has walked into a nice stack and just needs minor repositioning.

Step 2. Hold the bait in front of the dog's face and allow him to nibble on it as you reposition his legs. If his front feet are nicely placed, don't mess with them; correct the rear legs. If he sits down or moves around, say, "Uh-oh," and pull the food away and start over. It takes time for a dog who isn't used to having his legs positioned to become comfortable with the process.

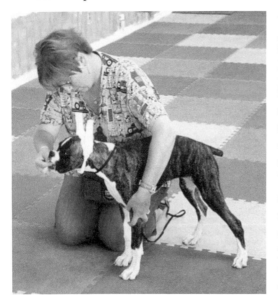

Work on this step until you can set him up easily. Don't worry about stay yet. If the dog is not used to being handled, this may take some time. A young or very active dog may need a lot of practice. Don't be frustrated. When he moves, say, "Uh-oh," the minute he moves, remove the bait and try again. Once the dog is comfortable standing while you reposition his legs, you can teach him to hold the stack.

Kaeli, a Boxer puppy, is learning to have her legs repositioned.

Step 3. Stack him, tell him, "Stay," then say, "Yes," and reward right away. Add a second or two before you say, "Yes," and reward. As he becomes more successful, build duration so he can hold the stay for as long as needed in the show ring, which is sometimes a couple minutes. If he moves before you say, "Yes," re-stack and don't give him a treat. If he keeps wiggling, say, "Oh well," and stop working for a few minutes. If you are using a desirable food reward, the dog will want to keep working.

Step 4: When the dog is reliable, add distractions. Practice in new and different locations.

Step 5: Once the dog can stack reliably and stay, vary the rewards. Continue to use food, but add praise, games and toys.

Chapter 8
THE EXAMINATION

Possibly the most important element of training a show dog is teaching him to accept a thorough examination by a judge—it can make or break a show dog's career. Your dog must learn to tolerate having his bite examined, being handled over his entire body, and not to wiggle too much during the process. You want a dog who not only accepts or tolerates handling by a judge, but also loves it. Two things you can do early on with your dog to accept examinations by a judge is early socialization and desensitization, the latter especially if your dog exhibits fear of being examined.

Here is a dog who is very comfortable being examined by a judge.

Early Socialization is the Key

It all starts with proper socialization. Any dog, show ring competitor or companion, deserves to be raised properly. There is a window of opportunity for this crucial training when pups are between seven and twenty weeks of age. You should be actively socializing your dog during this time period; in fact, for the entire first year. Begin socializing your puppy right away. I begin socializing my puppies as soon as I acquire them, which is usually at seven to eight weeks.

A dog who is properly socialized doesn't usually need much training to accept gentle handling. If the dog likes people, for the most part, he won't mind being examined by a judge. There are, of course, some breeds that do not love all people (particularly strangers), but they must still be willing to accept handling. Teaching the dog to stand still for examination is sometimes the biggest challenge, especially for friendly and outgoing dogs.

Most judges want to run their hands all over the dog. This means the head, muzzle, shoulders and chest, front legs, topline, hindquarters and rear legs. Male dogs must accept a stranger handling their testicles. Some breeds, such as the Pekingese, are lifted up so the judge can be sure the dog's body weight is distributed properly. These dogs need to be accustomed to this type of handling from a judge.

For more information on the benefits of early socialization and other training you can do with puppies, see Chapter 10.

Desensitization

Even if you do a good job of socializing your dog, he may still exhibit fear or discomfort with being examined by a judge. If this is the case with your dog, the best way to solve the problem is with desensitization. While there are many ways to do this, in positive dog training the process of desensitization usually involves introducing a trigger (whatever the dog fears or reacts badly to) at a very low intensity level. That trigger is then paired with something the dog likes, usually a high value treat. Feeding your fearful dog treats while a stranger slowly approaches and begins to pet him can be an effective use of desensitization.

For example, I desensitized Rodeo, an Australian Cattle Dog mix, who I rescued recently. Rodeo had absolutely no training (had never been in the house, didn't know his name and wasn't used to being handled). When I first tried to look in Rodeo's mouth or touch his feet, he would swing his head around and grab my hands with his mouth. He wasn't "biting," but he was mouthing me. If I had forced him without gradually desensitizing him, he probably would have bitten me.

Examining the Bite

A show dog must accept an examination of his bite. In some breeds, the judge may actually count teeth; in others, the judge just peeks inside. Whatever the case, your dog must be accustomed to someone looking in his mouth. Because there are different kinds of judges, be aware that some are incredibly kind and gentle, while others are fast and rough. It is important that your dog is used to being examined in a variety of ways so he isn't surprised in the ring.

Check your dog's bite everyday. By making this a routine, you teach him that checking his bite is a normal, everyday event. Choose a word to signal to the dog who you are going to examine his mouth. I tell my dogs and puppies, "Mouth please." When they are in the ring and the judge is going to look into the mouth, they won't be alarmed because I let them know what is about to happen.

To examine the mouth, simply place your hand over the dog's muzzle and use your thumb and middle finger to carefully lift up his lips. Have your fingers close enough to the front of the mouth so you (and eventually the judge) can see the front of the bite. Be calm and gentle. Release, and then praise your dog. Do this every day, several times a day if possible.

If you follow the steps above, your dog should tolerate having his bite examined by you and eventually a judge. If not, here is a sample training plan for desensitizing a dog to this procedure.

Step 1. Sit on the floor or the couch with your dog and pet him. If he is excited or jumpy, calmly wait until he settles down. Ignore him when he is overly excited; pet him softly when he is calm.

Step 2. Stroke your dog all over his body. Run your hand over the top of his muzzle, his head, and his back. Don't focus on the mouth yet. Just make the muzzle part of the petting process. Do this regularly until your dog enjoys being touched. Offer him a treat and verbal encouragement if he is calm while you touch him. Once your dog is calm and relaxed about this handling, move to Step 3.

Step 3. Sit on the floor or the couch like you did in Step 2. Pet your dog for about two minutes. Then, gently touch your dog's muzzle. Do not lift the lips or examine the bite at this time, just pet the muzzle. If he is calm, offer verbal praise. You can incorporate a food reward by offering treats between muzzle strokes. However, if you have a dog who goes crazy about food, a reward might be too stimulating and you may need to stick to verbal encouragement. See what works for your dog. Continue with this step until your dog is completely relaxed when you touch his muzzle.

Step 4. Next, put a treat in your right hand and pet him with the other. Hold the treat in front of his mouth so he can nibble on it; place your left hand over his muzzle while he eats the treat. Continue with this step until he ignores your hand over his muzzle.

Step 5. There are two options at this point. The first option is to allow the dog to nibble on a treat while you put your hand over his muzzle and lift his lips. Or, stash some treats nearby (not in your hand). Sit down as if you are going to pet the dog. Do this for a minute or two, then stroke the muzzle. As you pet the dog's muzzle, gently lift up one side of the dog's lips. Do not attempt to look inside his mouth. If he has his head down and he is relaxed, do not disturb him or move his head. Just lift the lip. If he accepts this easily, tell him how good he is and give him a treat. Continue working on this until your dog is comfortable with you lifting both sides of his mouth.

As noted, you can desensitize any body part using these steps. Take your time and don't rush. Pushing too fast causes the dog to regress, and you will have to start over. Once your dog is comfortable with you handling a certain body part, ask friends to do the same. Finally, have friends act as judges and touch your dog's entire body.

Gentle Handling

The following steps are for teaching a friendly, well-socialized dog to be able to accept handling. Dogs that like people and enjoy being handled probably won't have any problems, and you can move along quickly. If your dog is not comfortable being handled, desensitization may be necessary.

Step 1. While you are watching television or cuddling with your dog, gently run your hands over his entire body. Touch his body and legs. Touch each foot. Look into his ears and into his mouth. Do this every day.

Step 2. Once your dog is comfortable being touched, stack him and ask a family member to walk up to him as a judge would. Pretend that you are showing him and the other person is examining him. Have him stack and stay. If he wiggles or moves away while being examined, say, "Uh-oh." Have the person move away and stack him again. Once he settles down, have the person try again. You want the dog to learn that he receives attention only when he settles down.

Step 3. Stack your dog and have people unfamiliar to the dog walk over to him, similar to how a judge would. If your dog is friendly and outgoing, he may want to wiggle. Ask him to stand still. Use food to keep him steady if you have to.

If any part of the examination makes your dog nervous or uncomfortable, you will need to desensitize him before showing him. A judge does not want to examine a dog who is nervous or afraid. (As an exhibitor and breeder, I don't want to show a dog who seems nervous or afraid.) The judge doesn't know if the dog is nervous because he isn't well-socialized or if the nervousness is the result of genetic temperament. Either way, the dog probably won't win. Take time to make sure your dog is comfortable and relaxed about being examined.

Wiggles During Examination

Perhaps your small dog is not afraid of the table, but wiggles when the judge approaches. The positive solution to that problem is very different from the previous desensitization process. You have a dog that loves people. This is great—until you go to a dog show. What the dog wants is the judge, or anyone really, to touch and pay attention to him. He doesn't understand the difference between a friendly person petting him and a judge examining him. All he knows is that he likes both!

To solve this problem, you will need a table similar to that used at a dog show. You also need a few friends to help you.

Step 1. Place your dog on the table and set him up in a show stack. Ask a friend to approach the dog. If the dog doesn't move, say, "Yes," or click and treat, and then allow the person to pet him. If he moves, say "Uh-oh," and have the person take a step back and ignore the dog while you set him up again. Have the person step forward toward the dog again. If the dog moves, have the person step back, and you say, "Uh-oh." Try this three times. If the dog continues to wiggle each time, have the person go into another room for a few minutes, then try again. This is a very powerful technique. You are using negative punishment (removing something pleasant to the dog as a consequence for moving). Outgoing dogs are very frustrated when they are not allowed to visit. Once the dog realizes that in order to visit he has to remain still, he stays still.

Step 2. Take the table and the dog to a dog show or conformation class, and try the technique outlined in Step 1. Ask friends and strangers to approach your dog.

Do not enter the dog in shows until he masters standing still on the table when people approach. Remember the basic principle of positive training: if a behavior is reinforced, the dog is likely to repeat the behavior. If the dog wiggles when the judge walks up to examine him, the dog will be reinforced for wiggling since you can't ask the judge to step away. The dog must learn that he earns a reward when he stays still. And, if you are smart, you can sweeten the pot with a click and treat so he really learns to love it.

Chapter 9

POSITIVE SOLUTIONS TO DOG SHOW PREDICAMENTS

When a dog is not showing well, finding a positive solution means returning to the basic principles of how dogs learn, and it requires creativity on the part of the handler. You need to know what drives your dog, and then use that knowledge to help him improve. Remember, you can't force a dog to enjoy showing. You must figure out what will help him like it.

Depending on the problem or predicament, food may not be the answer. That's why you have to think carefully before proceeding. Following are a variety of techniques, all based on positive methods, which can be used to solve common problems. Your specific predicament may not be included, but these solutions may help you formulate a plan of your own.

Fear

The show environment—noise, strange people and dogs, activity, new surroundings—can be frightening to dogs. It is not unusual for show dogs to develop some kind of fear associated with showing. Sometimes you can pinpoint the cause of the fear, many times you cannot.

More important than figuring out the cause of your dog's fear is handling the fears delicately and correctly.

Fear-based problems should be corrected with positive reinforcement. It is unkind and unfair to insist that a frightened dog "Just deal with it" or

"Get over it." You have to be careful or you can ruin a dog (not only for the show ring, but also as a companion) by forcing him to do something that frightens him. Remember, frightened dogs are not "getting away" with anything. They aren't looking for a victory over you, they are just too afraid to do what you are asking. It's very important to look carefully at a dog's reactions. Do not assume that "He just doesn't want to do it" or he is "being stubborn." The dog that is labeled "stubborn" is often afraid or misunderstood.

Generally fear is best dealt with by using desensitization and counter-conditioning techniques. As explained in Chapter 8, desensitization is when you slowly desensitize the dog by introducing the triggers (what scares him) at a low level, and then counter-condition by giving him something he really likes in the presence of the trigger. Fear should dissipate as the dog experiences something pleasant in the presence of what causes fear. This technique of retraining a dog isn't used enough in the dog show world.

Fear of the Table

Many dogs are afraid of being placed on the show-ring examination table. It may be because of a fear of the judge, or being lifted and placed on a small surface high above the ground (high for a small dog!) If you show a dog who fears the table, follow the desensitization and counter-conditioning techniques described below.

Step 1. Fold up the table legs and lay the table on the ground so it is stable and only a few inches high. Fill your pocket or bait bag with treats the dog absolutely cannot resist. Entice the dog to the table by setting a treat on the table. If you are training with a clicker, click and treat when your dog goes near the table to collect the treat. If you aren't using a clicker, use a verbal marker such as, "Yes" or "Good boy."

Step 2. Once your dog moves near the table comfortably, use the treat to lure him onto the table. With the treat in your hand, move it over the table so that the dog must step on the table to receive the treat. Work on this step until the dog is happily hopping on the table for his treats. Don't force him on the table. Consider feeding his meals on the table to reinforce good "feelings" about the table.

Step 3. Next, set the table up to its full height. Carefully lift your dog onto the table and give him a treat. At this point, it's not important that he stacks. Your goal is to condition him to love being on the table. If your dog seems afraid, place the table against a wall, which can add a sense of security. Stick to this step until the dog is comfortable with the table. Once he is, feed his dinner on the table. Once the dog is comfortable on the table, work on stacking and examination as discussed in Chapters 7 and 8.

Story is being fed on the table to encourage her to enjoy it.

Fear of the Judge

Another common problem among show dogs is a fear of the judge. Typically, these dogs are fearful or suspicious of strangers, not just judges at dog shows. The solution is to deal with fear of all strangers and once again, desensitization and counter-conditioning is the way to do it. You must teach your dog that meeting strangers is fun and rewarding.

This process involves taking your dog on walks, and you will need the help of friends or neighbors. You will also need to be armed with your dog's favorite treats.

Step 1. Set up a scenario in which you walk your dog and a friend slowly approaches from a distance. When your dog notices your friend, feed the dog some treats. It doesn't matter at this point what the dog is doing because classical conditioning is at work in this instance. (Remember, classical conditioning means that the dog is learning strictly by association.) Your friend should not be close enough to cause stress in the dog—otherwise your friend is too close. The food is not contingent on the dog's behavior; it is being given to the dog in the presence of a trigger (the person) to change the dog's response to the trigger. It is important that the dog sees your friend before you give the food. The dog must learn that the person caused the food to be offered to him. Make sure that you are using a high-value reward when doing this. Once the person is gone, so is the irresistible food.

If your dog won't take the food, either the food isn't good enough or you are too close to approaching person, which causes the dog to be too stressed to eat. If that happens, have the person move back to a point where the dog accepts food, but is still able to see the person. Practice this often, and always give out a lot of treats. Make sure people don't unexpectedly walk up to your dog while you are working on this problem. Over time, you should notice your dog becoming more relaxed when he sees a person approaching. Your dog learns that when "scary" people appear, fantastic food comes out and when the person disappears, so does the food.

Step 2. Once the dog is comfortable with people at a distance, begin to slightly decrease the distance. As the dog associates the approach of a stranger with an attractive food reward, you should see the dog become excited at the sight of the trigger. Tolerating the person isn't enough; he needs to appear happy and excited.

Step 3. Next, the person approaches and offer treats to the dog. Don't rush this step. Your dog must be completely calm and relaxed around people before people touch him.

While approaching, have your friend ignore the dog (no talking to the dog, no eye contact), but as she gets closer she should toss treats toward him. Repeat this activity until the dog is comfortable. It is crucial to enlist good helpers who won't attempt to push the dog too fast.

Step 4. Now ask your friend to approach slowly, and then crouch down, still avoiding eye contact while maintaining a sideways position to the dog. When a dog is approached head on, he is more likely to find this threatening. To avoid that, have people approach from the side. Continue until the dog is comfortable with your friend touching him. It may take some time, but taking it slow is better for the dog in the long run.

Step 5. It is now time to generalize this behavior by repeating the same scenario with friendly strangers. Again, move slowly to ensure that the dog is really comfortable. Take your dog for a walk. Click and treat when people walk up to you, or walk by and your dog doesn't show signs of shyness or fear. If you are dedicated and consistent, most dogs will come along in a reasonable timeframe.

Notice how the dog is approached with the stranger sideways and with no direct eye contact. This position is much less threatening to the dog.

Step 6. Once your dog confidently approaches people, you can ask people to approach him as a judge would. Stack your dog and have a friend, then a stranger, approach him and examine him. If you have followed these steps carefully, your dog should be comfortable with this. If he seems nervous, use food to distract him until he learns to relax while being examined, or go back and repeat step 5. Continue to work on all of your show skills at home while you are going through this desensitization process. That way, when you are ready to show, he will already have all of the show training under his belt.

The key to overcoming fear is not pushing the dog beyond his limits before he is ready. Owners sometimes want to show the dog so badly they enter shows before the dog is ready and it causes real setbacks. Fight the urge to get the dog into the ring until the dog is truly comfortable with strangers in a variety of situations. You want your dog

Positive Training Tip

When desensitizing a dog, it is crucial to keep him at a "sub-threshold" level. For example, in the case of an approaching stranger, "sub-threshold" means that he is far enough away from the stranger so that he remains outwardly calm. However calm he appears, he may be actually fairly anxious. Watch his body language for signs of stress and keep him far enough away from the trigger to keep him from reacting badly.

to have a lifelong, positive effect from showing, not just a finished title. Your dog will let you know when he is ready to show.

Positive Training Tip

What triggers your dog's fear? Is it the judge? The table? The noise? Once you figure out what triggers the fear, you can desensitize the dog using the previously outlined steps. Some dogs have several fears. If this is the case, you must desensitize the dog one fear at a time. Do not show the dog while you are desensitizing him. This is frustrating for owners, but it's important. You don't want to push the dog before he is ready. If you do, it could exacerbate the fears.

Sitting When Coming Back to the Judge

Dogs trained to walk on a loose leash and sit, often sit instead of stand for examination by the judge. Teaching the dog to stand on command will solve this problem, and it's easy to teach. The clicker works especially well for this one.

Step 1. Arm yourself with the clicker and treats, and stand in front of the dog. If the dog is standing, click and treat. If the dog continues to stand, click and treat again. Continue to do this until the dog stands for at least a minute. If the dog sits, take a step directly toward

Notice the correct body position of the stranger approaching. This dog has graduated to accepting gentle petting on the head.

him—this is likely to cause him to stand again. As soon as he stands, click and treat. If he remains standing, click and treat again. However, if the dog does not stand, but remains sitting, take a step back, encouraging him to walk toward you. As soon as he stands, click and treat. It's important to remember to click immediately when he stands. Don't wait for the dog to hold a stand, or you will be waiting forever. You want to teach him that the standing position earns the clicks.

Step 2. Once the dog offers a stand, say the word, "Stand," or "Stack," just before you click and treat. As soon as he stands, click and treat. Once you cue the behavior, you can ask the dog to move, then come to a stop by saying, "Stand." Click and treat. If the dog does not stop and stand, say "Uh-oh," and try again. The treat comes only when the dog stands.

Step 3. Now that the dog knows how to refrain from sitting, practice in front of a mock judge. If he sits,

Practice approaching a mock judge.

have the "judge" move away and start again. Don't expect long stand-stays at first. In the beginning, just standing is a big deal. Once he stands reliably, then add duration.

Dogs who Show with Their Tails Down

Another common problem is the dog who shows with his tail down. If the breed is supposed to carry the tail high, over the back, but it's down, the dog isn't going to win. It is worth your time and effort to determine why the tail is down and figure out what you can do about it.

The dog's tail gives information. In canine body language, the carriage of the tail is part of how dogs read each other, and it can help you read your dog, too. Dogs tuck or drop their tails for many reasons including fear, insecurity, or a desire to "disappear" from the ring. Most dogs who tuck or drop their tails do it because they aren't comfortable in the ring. Why they are uncomfortable is often a mystery, but that doesn't really matter. Your job is to teach your dog how to relax and enjoy being in the ring.

Teaching a dog to keep his tail up in the ring begins by making sure all training and ring experiences are lighthearted and fun. Train with a prized toy or favorite treats. Enter fun matches to give both of you a better opportunity for a successful ring experience (fun matches are usually less stressful). Stay upbeat during training and at actual events.

Step 1. Institute training sessions dedicated to "Tail up" work. Observe what your dog is doing or reacting to when his tail is up and try to re-create those conditions. Click and treat any movement of his tail as long as it is up. Practice this often because you want to make sure the dog understands what you are clicking.

Step 2. Once the dog stands and moves with his tail up, add a cue such as, "Tail up," in an upbeat voice, followed by a click and treat.

Step 3. When your dog understands tail up, work on gaiting with the tail up. Make sure both behaviors are solid before moving on.

Step 4. Work with your dog in low-pressure environments, such as classes and fun matches. Praise and treat him lavishly for keeping his tail up. Once he is doing so reliably, it's time to put him in the show ring.

Kaeli is being clicked for her tail position. Notice that I am not too concerned with the rest of her body position; I am working solely on the "Tail up" command.

Dogs Who Show with Their Heads Down/Sniffing the Ground

Sniffing is a common sight in the show ring. There are two major reasons for sniffing. First, the dog sniffs because there are really interesting smells in that area. Also, the dog is anxious and sniffing is a stress reaction (for more information, read *On Talking Terms* With Dogs by Turid Rugaas, cited in the Resource section).

If your dog sniffs to calm his nerves, be sure you to follow the desensitization and counter-conditioning instructions given previously. Whatever you do, do not correct an anxious dog that sniffs because it simply makes him more anxious.

If your dog is primarily interested in the fascinating scents in the ring, take him to a local park or grassy area where there are a lot of interesting smells. Bring the most fabulous, high-value food rewards you can find, and move around with your dog. Any time the dog's nose is on the ground, turn in another direction. Any time that his nose comes up, click and treat. Your dog will learn quickly that keeping his head up is more rewarding than sniffing. Keep in mind that sniffing is a self-reinforcing behavior. This means that sniffing feels good to the dog and is a reward all by itself. That is why using a high-value treat is so important. The reward must be better than sniffing!

For the dog who doesn't hold his head high enough to show well, you can use your hand or a touch stick to teach your dog correct head position. You can teach the dog to keep his head up by asking him touch a stick or your hand as discussed in Chapter 6. If you decide to use your hand, simply replace the touch stick with your hand in these exercises.

Step 1. Teach your dog "Touch," as explained in Chapter 6. Begin this exercise in an area free of distractions, such as your backyard or in your home.

Step 2. Hold the leash in your left hand, and the clicker and touch stick in your right hand. Have treats readily available in a bait bag.

Step 3. Hold the touch stick so it goes across your body and the end of the stick is in front of your dog's nose. Take a step or two forward, cue the dog "Touch," allow your dog to touch the stick, then follow with a click and treat. Make sure the stick is positioned head high to help the dog keep his head up where you want it.

Using "Touch" to keep Rodeo's head up.

Step 4. Once your dog can follow the target stick for one or two steps, add more steps. Also, say, "Head up," just before you click and treat. It is important to put the behavior on cue so the dog can do it once you stop using the stick.

Step 5. Practice until your dog can follow the stick the distance of the ring with his head up. Then, practice without the stick.

Difficulty with Picture Taking

The camera shy dog is frustrating for handlers, especially if your dog has performed well in the ring and you want a great photo to help commemorate the occasion. There are several reasons why a dog may not respond well when posing for pictures. Many owners run out of the ring, frantically trying to gather their trophies and ribbons. They rush over to the show photographer for photos. More often than not, rushing about stresses the dog. If you are rushed and your dog is stressed, you won't get a good picture. Remember that when a dog has an owner who is anxious, he will feel anxious, too.

You must first relax and slow down. Make picture taking a relaxing and fun experience. Bring along your dog's favorite treats. If you used liver bait in the ring, bring steak for pictures. Don't rush to be first in line. Instead, go to the end of the line. This is helpful for two reasons. First, it allows your dog to settle down. Second, if you are last you don't feel as much pressure to rush through the process. While you are waiting, pet or massage your dog. Talk to him calmly.

Remain calm when setting up your dog for the photograph. Talk to your dog quietly. Position his legs gently and feed him the meat while you set him up. This is where owners and handlers go wrong. They feel stressed and rushed, and they throw their dog into position. This makes the dog anxious, so he moves, or slinks down. Slinking is a dog's way of saying he wants to disappear.

Whatever you do, don't choke up on the collar. I recently watched a novice handler do this. Her dog was fidgeting on the table when they were taking pictures. She had a choke collar and lead on the dog, and was holding it up high and tight. The dog was choking the entire time they were trying to snap a picture.

The dog couldn't hold still and relax because he couldn't breathe! I finally told her to release the collar or hold him by the collar so that it wasn't choking the dog. Finally, when she released, the dog stood still.

The following is a progression of steps to teach your dog to enjoy being photographed. If you have a large dog and don't use a table to show, follow the same procedure, just without the table.

Step 1. Arm yourself with a high-value food reward that your dog absolutely loves. It should be a treat the dog rarely gets, not even in the show ring. It must be incredibly delicious.

Step 2. Set your grooming table up in a quiet area with few distractions. Somewhere so you don't inadvertently add anxiety to the dog while you are practicing.

Step 3. With your table up and your high-value treat out, say a word to your dog such as, "Pictures," then pick him up and put him on the grooming table. If he remains calm, click and treat. Talk nicely, praising him as you give the food. You want him to love the table, and feel calm and relaxed while on it.

Step 4. Take your high-value treats with you to the dog show and bring them out only for picture time. You may use whatever treat you like in the ring, but reserve a very special treat for pictures.

All dog fanciers want great show photos. The truth is, some are great and others are stashed at the bottom of a desk drawer never to be seen. To make the most of picture time at shows, teach the dog to enjoy it. Work on stacking him quickly under pressure at home so it doesn't make him anxious at shows.

As an alternative, have photos taken elsewhere. No, the judge won't be in the picture, but if you want the picture for advertising, you can list the wins and judges in the text. Personally, I think portraits or dog photos with different, creative backgrounds are a refreshing touch in dog show magazines.

Conformation Classes—What to Watch For

Conformation classes are great if you want more training opportunities and/or to work on solving specific problems like those mentioned in this chapter. Conformation classes can also be disastrous. It all depends on the instructor, the other dogs in attendance, and your individual dog's temperament.

If you wish to attend a conformation class, find a class that uses positive reinforcement methods. This can be a challenging task. Unfortunately, most conformation classes use traditional training styles, although this is starting to change. This means that you might not see progressive, positive reinforcement methods as discussed in this book. Some classes may be a mix of both positive reinforcement and aversive methods. You may be encouraged to use food and positive reinforcement, as well as correction and force. Some instructors insist they are positive trainers and that their methods are positive, but still use choke chains and neck corrections.

If you are committed to using the positive reinforcement training methods recommended in this book, you must find a teacher who is aligned with your viewpoint. Your instructor's methods shouldn't be a guessing game. The techniques should be spelled out on their website or in printed material. If they aren't spelled out, ask questions to make sure you agree with his or her training methods.

It's best if you can observe a class before signing up. Observing a class gives you an opportunity to watch the instructor teach and see firsthand how the classes are run, the methods used and the instructor's teaching style. Viewing a class before participating is particularly important if you have a sensitive dog. You need to see how the class is run, check out the building and location, and the other dogs in attendance. Some instructors emphasize the importance of not allowing the dogs to visit and socialize, while some will pay little or no attention to this at all. All of these are important factors in helping you decide if this is where you want to take conformation class.

Some conformation classes offer almost no instruction, but are geared toward just having the dog practice being shown. These classes are good for positive trainers because you won't have to worry about being coerced into a training style with which you don't agree.

In addition to choosing an instructor based on her training methods and beliefs, you want to assess her "people" skills. A great dog trainer is not necessarily a great people trainer. A good teacher must be talented at teaching people. After all, the owners that attend a dog training class want training for themselves so they can in turn train their dogs.

Consider the size of the classes and the training facility. In general, small class sizes are better. While easy-going and well-adjusted dogs may tolerate a large class, dogs who are new to showing, insecure, or shy may find a large class stressful. Six to ten dogs per class is probably the right size. The building can be a factor. For a normal, outgoing, well-socialized dog, the building won't matter too much. However, an indoor class in a building with poor acoustics can echo and be frightening to fearful dogs. Visiting the class gives you a chance to check all this out to determine if the class will be beneficial to your dog.

Instructors vary in how much instruction they give and how much time is ring practice. A lot of ring practice in a conformation class is fairly typical. What this means is that many classes do not give much, if any, instruction, but focus on practicing for a dog show. This may be all your dog needs. If this is the case, a conformation class is icing on the cake.

If you decide that you have done what you can on your own and you want to work on ring practice, a conformation class with a flexible, positive trainer can be incredibly helpful. Just do your homework. Observe the class, talk to the instructor beforehand and be informed about how she trains.

Chapter 10
RAISING GOOD SHOW DOGS

It is interesting to consider what it takes to raise a successful show dog. The behavioral aspects of a good show dog are exactly the same traits that make a good pet. Both should be well-socialized, relaxed, and comfortable around people and dogs. It is a plus if your show dog is friendly and outgoing, but this varies among individual dogs and breeds.

Show dog or not, all dogs deserve to be raised properly.

It is best to acquire your show dog as a puppy (assuming you did not breed him yourself) so you can begin training early. It also gives you the opportunity to make sure he is properly socialized.

Socialization

Advising you to socialize your puppy seems obvious, but it is surprising how many owners don't take the time to adequately socialize their puppies. Some owners, even experienced breeders, assume that if you have other dogs around, the puppy will get socialized by osmosis! Or, they think that periodic visitors will accustom the puppy to all kinds of people. Puppies need to be socialized with dogs (of different breeds and ages), men, women, teenage boys, teenage girls, young boys and girls, cats, cars, strangers and anything or anyone else an adult dog might be exposed to later in life. A puppy will not receive adequate socialization by staying at home.

Of course, there is the dog who is naturally easygoing and gets by on haphazard socialization, but this is rare. It simply isn't worth taking the chance. All puppies—show and companion—deserve to be raised so they will become well-adjusted adult dogs or they won't be welcome members of society .

The truth is it takes a great deal of thought and effort to do a good job of socializing a dog. Raising a puppy is like raising a child. Every experience in that puppy's life is a training opportunity. You must be committed to making sure that your dog's puppyhood is full of positive, varied, and happy experiences. You want the same cheerful, friendly, outgoing temperaments for companion dogs and show dogs.

Unfortunately, there are breeders who keep puppies as show prospects and do no socializing or training with them. Then, if the dog doesn't turn out to be show material, they have an unruly, under-socialized "pet" dog that needs placement. Many times the breeder's attitude is that the new owner should feel lucky to get one of her dogs. No reputable breeder should ever place a dog that isn't properly socialized. Remedial socialization is a difficult task, and it isn't fair to the dog or to the new owners.

Keep in mind that despite adequate or even outstanding socialization, some dogs are uncomfortable with people. This is a topic that requires its own book because training shy dogs can be a daunting job. On the other hand, well-socialized shy dogs are usually much easier to rehabilitate than shy dogs with no socialization. The message here is this: do your best to socialize your pup and you are headed in the right direction.

Show Dog Socialization
The process you follow to socialize your show dog depends if you are the breeder or if you acquire the puppy from someone else. Whatever the case, you should work on socializing, and most experts agree that the prime window of opportunity for this is about seven to twenty weeks of age. The time frame varies among individual dogs, but you can't afford to wait until the dog is six months old to begin the process. Start early, and be wary of acquiring an unsocialized puppy older than six months.

As with any puppy, expose your show puppy to as many life experiences as you can. There are several areas on which to focus for the future show dog:

1. Crowds and congested areas that include people and dogs

2. Long drives in a vehicle

3. Being comfortable in a crate or exercise pen

4. Sudden and strange noises as the dog might hear at a dog show

5. Handling by strangers.

This is Billy at a canine Halloween party when he was 4 months old. Fun get-togethers with well-socialized, vaccinated adult dogs can be great for puppies.

Be sure to keep all experiences lighthearted and positive. If you have a puppy that seems shy, be careful not to force or push too quickly. Let the puppy help decide when he is ready to be petted or receive a treat from a stranger.

When the discussion of puppy socialization comes up, the question of transmittable diseases and your pup's safety is likely to come up, as well. Here is my take on it. Be smart about where you take your puppy. Some veterinarians warn against taking your puppy out before he is 4 months old and has completed his initial vaccination protocol, but most veterinarians also agree that it is possible to socialize your puppy and still be safe about it. Take your pup to puppy classes or play groups where vaccination records are checked on all the dogs. Take him to friends' homes where there are friendly, vaccinated dogs to interact with. Do not take your puppy to dog parks or pet supermarkets. Do not let him run loose or sniff around other dog's feces or urine. Keep in mind, I see more dogs euthanized due to behavioral problems stemming from a lack of socialization than euthanized due to diseases. It is important to keep your puppy safe, but find ways to make sure he gets the socialization he needs.

Crate Training

Regardless if a puppy is a show prospect or a pet, crate training is a wise idea. Crate training helps with day-to-day training, as well as housetraining. However, crate training is essential for your show puppy because he will undoubtedly spend time in a crate at dog shows, and in a crate traveling to and from dog shows. The earlier becomes used to the crate the better.

The crate should be large enough for the puppy to stand up and turn around, but no bigger. Let your puppy adjust to being in the crate. As he becomes more accustomed to it, leave him for longer periods of time. Make the crate a positive experience for the puppy. Toss treats in the crate to encourage the puppy to go inside. Feed meals in the crate; this is sure to create a positive association. Use the crate as a quiet place for the puppy to enjoy a special treat or toy. The crate can be used for cool down or time-out periods (3-5 minutes only), but the pup should never be yelled at in the crate or put into the crate roughly. This will ensure he views his crate as a safe, fun place to go.

Housetraining

Never physically correct a puppy when housetraining. In fact, do not reprimand a puppy for an "accident." If the puppy makes a mistake, the owner wasn't watching closely. Puppies must be watched at all times when they are being housetrained. Preventing mistakes will make the job of housetraining much easier. If you see your puppy going potty in the house, simply say, "Uh-uh, outside," and rush him outside. Yelling or hitting the puppy teaches him that going potty near you is bad news. Thereafter, you may have a difficult time getting him to go in your presence. Reprimanding after the fact doesn't work. The key to successful housetraining is supervising the puppy at all times, take him out often and praise him when he gets it right.

Teach your puppy to go potty on cue. A show dog is frequently on the road, staying in strange places like hotels or RV parks. And, you want to avoid the embarrassment of your dog relieving himself in the ring. To train your puppy, select a cue to use when you take the puppy outside, such as, "Go potty." When the puppy starts to go, say, "Go potty," and reward him with a treat. You can clicker train this behavior, too. Wait until he is almost finished going, or the click may cause him to stop to run over for a treat! Once your puppy is trained to go on cue, it will make your life much easier when traveling to, or exhibiting at, dog shows.

Check out the book by Ian Dunbar in the Resources section for more housetraining advice. You can keep training fun and positive for you and your puppy.

Begin Training Early

Begin training your puppy right away. I have clicker-trained litters of puppies as young as three weeks old, the age at which many experts believe a dog is capable of learning. By two months of age, they were conditioned to the clicker and learning. So start them off on the right foot, nice and early!

Since the positive dog training techniques you have learned are all dog friendly, there is no down-side to training immediately. The sooner the better—young puppies are like sponges. They soak up all the information you have to give them. No matter what you are training a dog for, it is always best to start as early as possible. Positive training allows you to do that. When a puppy reaches six or seven months old, he is already approaching adolescence, which means training can be more difficult because by then he has developed habits (both good and bad) and has become more independent.

Puppy Preschool Classes

Puppy classes are a great place for your pup to learn basic behaviors, and they are a great way to for your puppy to interact with other puppies and people. Not all puppy classes are created equal. As the owner of a dog training/behavior consulting business, I love teaching puppy classes and encourage all inquiring puppy owners to sign up for my preschool classes. I encourage you to do that, but I advise you to do your homework to make sure you enroll in a class that will be a positive experience.

Here is how I organize my puppy preschool classes. While the classes in your area may be different than mine, you can use this information as a guide when judging whether the classes offered in your community will meet your needs.

Each session is six weeks long, and each class is divided into three parts: off leash play; puppy raising issues; and training.

Dottie learns to target my hand in puppy preschool class.

The class begins with fifteen to twenty minutes of off-leash play. The puppies are grouped so they only play off leash with dogs who are equal in size and/or temperament.

It is important that puppy play is supervised, and you need a qualified trainer to make sure the play is safe and fun for all the puppies. Some trainers allow puppies to "work it out between themselves," but this is not a good experience for many puppies, particularly shy ones. If a puppy is continually trying to get away from other dogs or is constantly stressed, then he is not getting the socialization and playtime he needs. Puppies that are upset by group play should be removed.

After play time, owners and pups sit down and we discuss a particular puppy-raising issue, such as biting, housetraining, crate training, feeding, grooming and so on.

We spend the last part of the class working on a beginning obedience behavior, using the clicker to teach it. In puppy class I teach sit, down,

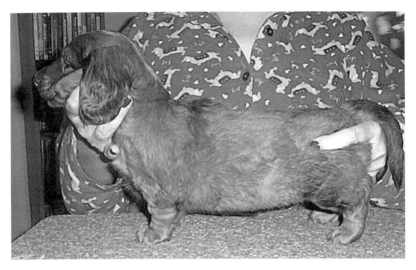

A puppy should always be handled gently to feel safe and secure.

come here, loose-leash walking, out, off, touch and leave it. Some people are concerned about teaching a show dog to sit, but I don't worry about that. Dogs are smart enough to learn both. You simply teach the dog to stand when you say, "Stand," and to sit when you say, "Sit."

The outline of my puppy class is just one way to do it. I have found this format to be very effective, but it doesn't mean it is the only way. I do think that some off-leash play time is important. Owners need to learn what appropriate puppy play is and what behaviors may be red flags.

Find a class whose instructor is committed to positive training methods. Despite what a few traditional trainers may tell you, it is entirely possible to train a dog without using corrections. Believe it or not, I know of trainers who start all puppies on an electronic remote (shock) collar. The good part is that many of those clients end up contacting a different trainer, but their dogs have sometimes already developed behavioral problems as a result of the shock collars. The sad part is that dogs who are trained with force must learn how to trust again, and many owners later feel guilty for having subjected their dogs to aversive training. The plain fact is there is no place for physical corrections when training a puppy. Remember that strong relationships are built on trust, understanding and communication, not intimidation and fear. Find a trainer who wants to help you build a strong, positive foundation for your puppy.

A Few No-Nos

No matter what anyone tells you, please do not put a choke chain on your puppy. It isn't necessary. A choke chain is designed to give control by creating an unpleasant feeling to the dog. This is not necessary with adult dogs and it is criminal with puppies. There are plenty of humane pieces of equipment that will help you get the job done. If you need that type of control—especially with a show dog—you need to work harder on your relationship with your dog. If you have to resort to a choke chain, then your relationship isn't balanced and it isn't strong.

Never pretend to drop a puppy off the back of a table. This is a major pet peeve of mine. I see breeders who think they know it all do this. Their "theory" and justification for this is that the puppy will be frightened and stand still. However, there are much kinder and more humane ways of teaching a puppy. I have dogs who stand still on the table and I never pretend to drop them off the table or handle them roughly. I am amazed at the lack of compassion some people show puppies.

The problem is that while many breeders understand structure and conformation, they know very little about canine behavior and learning. A good handler takes time to teach the puppy in a way that is comfortable and calming to the puppy. Good trainers don't have to frighten dogs to get what they want. Remember, good relationships aren't built on fear. They are built on trust. Teach your puppy to trust you, not be suspicious of you.

Keep your show dog's puppyhood positive and rewarding. Teach him to be outgoing and confident. Trust him when he shows he is frightened or insecure. Be patient, and help him with understanding. This will help to ensure a well-adjusted, confident adult dog who is willing and happy to partner with you.

Chapter 11

SUCCESS STORIES

When you decide to cross over to positive training, actually making the change can be challenging. You might be frustrated if positive training doesn't work right away, and be tempted to return to old training methods (force or punishment). You might also feel like giving up. Don't despair! Many owners face the same challenges. Following are some common problems, along with solutions, which made these dogs successful in the show ring. Let these stories be an encouragement to you.

Case #1

Dog: Paige, eight-month-old bitch

Problem: Fear, lack of socialization

Solution: Desensitization and counter-conditioning
Paige is a young bitch who was acquired as a show prospect at eight months of age. Her breeder said she was well-socialized, but in reality the only socialization she received was at dog shows, being moved from crate to crate, and from ex-pen to ex-pen.

Her new owner soon discovered that the Paige had many behavioral problems. She was afraid of the owner's husband, and was also fearful toward strangers. She was highly sound sensitive, fearful of different locations, not potty-trained or crate-trained, and incredibly insecure and anxious.

Paige exhibited a rock solid stand on the examining table by the breeder who sold her, but she was upset and would attempt to get away when examined in the breed ring. She was unable to remain calm anywhere except in the owner's home.

Paige's owner was afraid that she might not be able to finish the bitch due to behavioral problems. And, friends were questioning the owner's reasoning for keeping the dog and suggested she return it to the breeder. This was not an option because the owner bonded to the dog and was determined to keep her.

Upon meeting and observing Paige, I put together a treatment plan based on desensitization and counter-conditioning, which is the best way to deal with nearly all fear-based problems. We began with the grooming table. I recommended putting the dog on the grooming table at home and feeding her. Paige loves her owner and constantly seeks attention from her, so the owner's attention became a key reinforcement to her.

In a rather short period of time, Paige was able to sit on the grooming table, eat, and feel somewhat relaxed. Once the dog was comfortable on the table at home, I had the owner take a grooming table to shows and set it up outside the show ring. Then she fed the dog and paid attention to her while on the table. Once Paige was comfortable on the table at shows, we asked exhibitors to approach her and touch her gently (but no eye contact). Her owner was welcome to comfort her if she was nervous. We also had Paige attend a conformation class to desensitize her to the stimulus that terrified her. I asked her owner to take her to shows, but not to show her. Being examined by a judge might have pushed her beyond her comfort level and caused a setback.

The progress in Paige was phenomenal. Within weeks, she improved. At first, Paige wouldn't eat even high-value food rewards from her owner or others at dog shows. After a few shows, she was able to eat some treats from her owner and, even more astonishing, from strangers. She has since gone on overnight stays with a friend when her owner was on vacation, has learned to approach strangers (including men) visiting her house, has learned to remain much calmer at dog shows, and be examined by judges and finished her championship.

Can you imagine how sad it would be if the owner had sent Paige back to the breeder, as several people recommended? Without a doubt, Paige will continue to improve.

Case #2

Dog: Red, a "social butterfly"

Problem: Won't stand still for examination

Solution: Negative punishment

What do you do with a big, friendly show dog that loves people so much he can't stand still for examination? While the owner did a fabulous job socializing this dog, and the breeder bred a dog with a fine temperament, he is still a dog who will fail in the ring. Red is what I call a "social butterfly," a dog so friendly with people that he cannot be still while a judge examines him.

At first glance, a typically positive solution might be to skip a meal before the show, and use treats to try to get him to hold still. The problem is that to this dog, people are more reinforcing than food. Trainers who use compulsion might recommend that the owner pinch the dog's cheek or other body parts to get him to hold still, which I strongly discourage because it can turn a friendly, outgoing dog into an aggressive dog once he associates pain with approaching people.

Red's treatment plan was very simple and straightforward, and based on negative punishment. Remember that negative punishment means you take away something the dog finds reinforcing. For Red, approaching people was very reinforcing to him. So, rather than try to wrestle him into standing still, I asked his owner to stack him and then allow someone to approach. If he broke his stack, we asked the person approaching him to immediately turn and walk away while the owner said, "Too bad." This is extremely frustrating to a very social dog. He wants to meet people, unlike the bitch in Case #1. However, Red had to learn that people only approach if he holds the stack.

Once Red held still for examination, I reinforced that behavior with a treat. We practiced at dog shows to ensure success before facing an actual judge. This solution worked really well for Red. After a few weeks of training, Red responded and stood still for the judge. Red learned that the consequence for wiggling is people do not approach and pet him. The consequence for being still is being touched and receiving treats. I am confident that Red will continue to improve now that he is reinforced for the proper behavior.

Case #3

Dog: Dancer, a young champion

Problems: Fear of having photo taken

Solution: Classical conditioning using positive reinforcement

Dancer is a young, male champion. At a fairly young age, Dancer already had an impressive show career. His problem was common to many show dogs: he was afraid of being photographed. What do you do with a show dog that garners many wins, but the owner can't get a decent photograph because the dog slinks down, cringes and attempts to hide? This is a perfect example of the necessity of positive training with show dogs. This is a case in which you cannot force the dog to look good and be comfortable. You have to teach, and take your time doing it.

Dancer's owner told me the dog did great on the table in the show ring; it is only for pictures that he sank down and acted as though he hated showing. Show pictures are taken in a rush, and under pressure. Many exhibitors are waiting in line, the judge wants to go eat or get on to the next breed, and you need to get a fabulous picture. The owner sets up the dog quickly, and in a bit of a frenzy. The dog senses the tension, slinks down, attempts to "disappear" and appease the handler who is growing frustrated with the dog. Then the owner pulls the dog up and begins to get even more frustrated; the dog slinks even lower showing he is submissive. The scenario is common, and it is really frustrating to people who want nice pictures.

First, I asked Dancer's owner not to rush to the picture area. I asked her to remain relaxed and speak calmly to Dancer, then go to the end of the line for pictures so that she didn't think people were waiting and she could take her time setting him up. When she finally did put Dancer on the table for pictures, she was instructed to do it calmly, and not rush or yank Dancer around.

The solution to Dancer's problem was positive reinforcement and conditioning the dog to associate picture taking with treats. We were lucky that Dancer really likes food. I recommended that the owner determine Dancer's favorite food reward. I didn't care what the food was, even if it was marinated steak. It had to be his absolute favorite and it would only be used for picture time. I instructed her to give a word for the food reward. Every time the owner gave Dancer that food reward she would say, "Pictures," in a happy, cheerful voice and give the dog the treat. She was to practice this until the word "Pictures" made the dog very excited.

Once Dancer was familiar with the routine and enjoyed the game, I asked his owner to put him on the table, say the word and give him the treat. Next, she was to stack him while giving him the treats.

When it came time for a dog show, I gave Dancer's owner specific instructions about picture time. I told her to bring the favorite treat that she used with the word "Pictures." This treat was to be used only for pictures, not in the show ring. With these techniques in hand Dancer's owner has been able to get some nice show photos of Dancer—and they are continuing to improve.

Case #4

Dog: Maggie, puppy bitch

Problems: Showing with nose to the ground

Solution: Desensitization and counter-conditioning
Maggie is a great dog, a beautiful puppy with a nose for hunting. While her owner intended to train the dog for field trials, she also wanted to finish her conformation championship. However, it difficult to finish a dog when her nose is on the ground! Dogs that sniff, especially at times that do not seem logical, are usually stressed. A dog who sniffs excessively in the ring may not be doing it just to sniff, he may be doing it to look inconspicuous. Other dogs genuinely enjoy sniffing the ground. This is a self-reinforcing act.

Using a leash to correct a sniffing dog can actually have the opposite effect that is intended. If the dog is sniffing out of stress and trying to disappear, correcting the dog is likely to make it worse.

In Maggie's case, she wasn't stressed or uncomfortable. She simply enjoyed sniffing. Maggie's excessive sniffing was corrected using a several techniques. First, I clicker trained her and rewarded her for walking with her head up on her own. I also taught Maggie to touch with a target stick. Every time she touched, she received a click and treat. I asked her to touch, move a few steps, then click and treat when she walked the few steps. As she became successful at just a step or two, I added duration, meaning she took a few more steps before clicking and treating. Before long, Maggie was cheerfully walking along with her head up.

Case #5

Dog: Ryan, a 6-month-old sighthound

Problems: Resists repositioning from the side

Solution: Proper handler body position
I recently had an interesting case with Ryan, a soft-tempered sighthound. Ryan would swing out, perpendicular to his owner when she went to stack him after moving in the ring. The puppy would move away so he was facing his owner whenever she would attempt to reposition him from the side. For this owner, it felt natural to her to stack him while standing over him. Ryan developed a habit of swinging out when his owner went to either free-stack or hand-stack him.

First, I taught Ryan to watch his owner's finger when she stopped. I taught him to stop wherever she put her hand. He would hold position temporarily, but eventually would swing out again. I improved the swinging by saying, "Uh-oh," and turning a circle away from him that would force him to reposition. However, Ryan would wiggle out and face her when she went to stack him with her hands.

Sometimes when I am working with a dog, it helps me to take the dog and work him by myself to get a feeling for what is bothering him. When I tried to hand stack Ryan, I realized he was more comfortable if I repositioned him from a kneeling position; I didn't lean over him. If I kneeled beside him and gently repositioned his legs by moving my hands under his body rather than over his body, he would stay in front of me and allow me to stack him. I found the same to be true when his owner stacked him. Ryan's problem with swinging out improved once I realized that his handlers needed to position themselves differently in order for him to stand still comfortably.

Hampton, one of my favorite client dogs, after winning a specialty show Best of Variety.

RESOURCES

Recommended Reading

As an avid reader, I have an extensive collection of books on training, showing, behavior and dogs in general. The list below contains some of my favorites and the ones that I think would be helpful for dog show people to have in their libraries. I recommend you check them out and take from them what will be helpful for you and your dog.

Going for the Blue: Inside the World of Show Dogs and Dog Shows, Roger A. Caras. A must read about dog shows. Explains how they work and what to expect.

Another Piece of the Puzzle: Puppy Development, Pat Hastings and Erin Ann Rouse. This book that talks about raising puppies, puppy stages, development, etc.

Raising a Champion, A. Meredith John and Carole L. Richards. This is a great resource for information on dog shows and how they work. Explains what to wear, how to enter, and more.

Getting Started with Clicker Training, Karen Pryor. This book explains how clicker training works. Nice intro book.

Click for Joy!, Melissa Alexander. A book on clicker training. Written in question and answer form, very helpful for beginning clicker trainers.

Bones Would Rain From The Sky, Suzanne Clothier. A great book about dog/human relationships.

The Other End of the Leash, Patricia McConnell, PhD. This book explains how dogs learn. Very helpful in understanding behavior.

The Cautious Canine, Patricia McConnell, PhD. This book talks about dealing with fear issues in dogs.

Fiesty Fido, Patricia McConnell, PhD. This book deals with on-leash dog aggression and reactivity.

Before and After You Get Your Puppy, Dr. Ian Dunbar. Helpful book on raising a puppy. Includes info on housetraining, etc.

The Culture Clash, Jean Donaldson. Explains how dogs learn. Very useful book.

Positive Perspectives, Pat Miller. Useful book on positive training in general.

Stress in Dogs, Martina Scholz and Clarissa von Reinhardt. This book teaches people to learn to read stress signals in dogs.

On Talking Terms With Dogs, Turid Rugaas. Another book about reading stress signals in dogs.

Websites

www.dogwise.com A great resource for dog books, including all of the ones on the book resource list.

www.sitstay.com Offers dog training supplies such as clickers, healthy treats and more.

www.clickertraining.com Offers clicker training supplies such as various styles of clickers, target sticks and more.

www.apdt.com is the Association of Pet Dog Trainers website. This website lists dog trainers and may be helpful in finding a positive reinforcement dog trainer. However, please be sure to ask questions, observe a class and do your homework before committing to a trainer.

www.akc.org is the American Kennel Club website where you can find entry forms, official rules and upcoming shows.

www.mbdca.org is the Mixed Breed Dog Club of America website for people interested in competing with mixed breeds.

Email Discussion List

Clickershowdogs is the author's email discussion list on clicker training and positive training for show dogs on yahoogroups.com

Acknowledgments

Thank you to my husband Rick for helping me to make my dreams come true. To my Dad for always believing in me. To my brother Matt, for being my creative inspiration. To my brother Mike for your constant love and support. And to my families, the Aquinos, the Ronchettes and the Esmeyers for always supporting whatever I choose to do.

Thank you to the trainers who inspire me; Denise Laberee, my first trainer ever. Christina Southworth, the best assistant anyone could hope for. Dawn Bushong, for helping me find my way. To Lisa Clifton-Bumpass and Lorril Gammon Fong-Jean (and the javadawgers) for accepting me into your group of friends and making me feel welcome. Thank you to my dog friends who understand my obsession; Crista O'Hara, Sheila Paske, Sharon Carr, Georgie Hesse, Rhonda Perkins, Linda Blain, Colleen Pepper, Michelle Wolff, Sherry Fischer, Jeff and Amy Thomas, Kathy King and Jennifer Anderson. Thank you to Dr. George Marmolejo and the staff of Chabot Veterinary Hospital. Thank you to my clients who allow me to learn from their dogs every day and to those clients who allowed me to photograph you and/or your dogs for this book. They are Katie and "Murphy" (Cavalier), Kelli Danielson and "Ginger" (Boston Terrier), Sheila Paske and "Story" (Dachshund), Sharon Carr and "Cap'n Jack" (Dachshund), Mary Christy and "Cleo" (American Staffordshire Terrier) and Karen Fink and "Dora" and "Rex" (Silken Windhounds) Melissa and Alan Reyes and "Kaeli" (Boxer), Georgie Hesse and "Hampton" (Dachshund), and Claudia Holaday and "J.R." (Dachshund), Kathy and Diane with "Josie" (Border Collie) and Lisa and Lorril with "Dottie" (American Pit Bull Terrier). Thank you to Larry, Charlene and Nate Woodward who believed in this project. Finally, thank you to my own dogs Slater, Ivy, Lester, Winnie, Billy, Ribbon and Cowboy for your unwavering patience and honesty.

One more word about pictures. You may have noticed some photographs of mixed breeds in this book. Mixed breeds can also compete in conformation (with the Mixed Breed Dog Club of America). I do rescue and during the time I was writing this book I would teach some of the show dog techniques to the rescue dogs so that the pictures would actually reflect a dog learning the behaviors.

Author Biography

Vicki Ronchette has been working with dogs professionally for over 22 years. She began focusing on training and behavior in the late 1980s when she was training her own dogs for competition obedience. Vicki is a Certified Pet Dog Trainer and the owner of *Braveheart Dog Training* in San Leandro, California. Vicki is involved in Dachshund and Cattle Dog rescue and competes with her dogs in conformation, earthdog, field trials, obedience and rally-o and also handles show dogs for other people. Vicki lives with her husband Rick and their five Dachshunds and two Cattle Dogs in San Leandro, California.

INDEX

Notes:

Notes:

BEHAVIOR & TRAINING

ABC's of Behavior Shaping; Fundamentals of Training; Proactive Behavior Mgmt, DVD. Ted Turner

Aggression In Dogs: Practical Mgmt, Prevention & Behaviour Modification. Brenda Aloff

Am I Safe? DVD. Sarah Kalnajs

Behavior Problems in Dogs, 3rd ed. William Campbell

Brenda Aloff's Fundamentals: Foundation Training for Every Dog, DVD. Brenda Aloff

Bringing Light to Shadow. A Dog Trainer's Diary. Pam Dennison

Canine Body Language. A Photographic Guide to the Native Language of Dogs. Brenda Aloff

Clicked Retriever. Lana Mitchell

Dog Behavior Problems: The Counselor's Handbook. William Campbell

Dog Friendly Gardens, Garden Friendly Dogs. Cheryl Smith

Dog Language, An Encyclopedia of Canine Behavior. Roger Abrantes

Evolution of Canine Social Behavior, 2nd ed. Roger Abrantes

Give Them a Scalpel and They Will Dissect a Kiss, DVD. Ian Dunbar

Guide To Professional Dog Walking And Home Boarding. Dianne Eibner

Language of Dogs, DVD. Sarah Kalnajs

Mastering Variable Surface Tracking, Component Tracking (2 bk set). Ed Presnall

My Dog Pulls. What Do I Do? Turid Rugaas

New Knowledge of Dog Behavior (reprint). Clarence Pfaffenberger

On Talking Terms with Dogs: Calming Signals, 2nd edition. Turid Rugaas

On Talking Terms with Dogs: What Your Dog Tells You, DVD. Turid Rugaas

Positive Perspectives: Love Your Dog, Train Your Dog. Pat Miller

Predation and Family Dogs, DVD. Jean Donaldson

Really Reliable Recall. Train Your Dog to Come When Called, DVD. Leslie Nelson

Right on Target. Taking Dog Training to a New Level. Mandy Book & Cheryl Smith

Stress in Dogs. Martina Scholz & Clarissa von Reinhardt

The Dog Trainer's Resource: The APDT Chronicle of the Dog Collection. Mychelle Blake (*ed*)

Therapy Dogs: Training Your Dog To Reach Others. Kathy Diamond Davis

Training Dogs, A Manual (reprint). Konrad Most

Training the Disaster Search Dog. Shirley Hammond

Try Tracking: The Puppy Tracking Primer. Carolyn Krause
Visiting the Dog Park, Having Fun, and Staying Safe. Cheryl S. Smith
When Pigs Fly. Train Your Impossible Dog. Jane Killion
Winning Team. A Guidebook for Junior Showmanship. Gail Haynes
Working Dogs (reprint). Elliot Humphrey & Lucien Warner

HEALTH & ANATOMY, SHOWING
An Eye for a Dog. Illustrated Guide to Judging Purebred Dogs. Robert Cole
Annie On Dogs! Ann Rogers Clark
Canine Cineradiography DVD. Rachel Page Elliott
Canine Massage: A Complete Reference Manual.
Jean-Pierre Hourdebaigt
Canine Terminology (reprint). Harold Spira
Dog In Action (reprint). Macdowell Lyon
Dogsteps DVD. Rachel Page Elliott
Performance Dog Nutrition: Optimize Performance With Nutrition.
Jocelynn Jacobs
Puppy Intensive Care: A Breeder's Guide To Care Of Newborn Puppies. Myra
Savant Harris
Raw Dog Food: Make It Easy for You and Your Dog. Carina MacDonald
Raw Meaty Bones. Tom Lonsdale
Shock to the System. The Facts About Animal Vaccination...
Catherine O'Driscoll
The History and Management of the Mastiff. Elizabeth Baxter & Pat Hoffman
Work Wonders. Feed Your Dog Raw Meaty Bones. Tom Lonsdale
Whelping Healthy Puppies, DVD. Sylvia Smart

Dogwise.com is your complete source for dog books on the web!

2,000+ titles, fast shipping, and excellent customer service.